Imagining the Future Museum

Imagining the Future Museum

21 Dialogues with Architects

András Szántó

HATJE
CANTZ

For Alanna

Contents

WONDER & HUMILITY: BUILDING THE TWENTY-FIRST-CENTURY ART MUSEUM

Two years ago, in 2020, in the depths of the Covid-19 pandemic, I sat down with art-museum directors to talk about how museums were evolving. The conversations, which were gathered in *The Future of the Museum: 28 Dialogues*, described how museums were adapting to a changing society. They were, in a sense, running on new software—becoming more open, inclusive, welcoming, participatory, technologically savvy, community-minded, and globally engaged.

But an art museum that runs on new software will need new hardware. Which is why I spent the spring and summer of 2022 talking with architects from around the world.

The Pendulum Is Swinging

If you are like me, you grew up with museums that were grand and imposing, radiating institutional authority—with architecture to match. More than a few looked like Greek temples, suggesting a cultural link that felt fabricated and overbearing, even to me, a European. For much of humanity, such Eurocentric connotations seemed distant at best, and reminders of extractive imperial histories at worst.

As a rule, women were absent from the stone-carved lists of artists' names lining the façades of these temples of art. Gaining entrance called for a sacrifice. One had to ascend a hill or flights of steps just to get to the front door (it was almost always a single entrance, and often a surprisingly small door). Inside, a mood of hushed solemnity prevailed. Guards watched every move. Viewing art consisted of walking silently in lockstep from one work to another, gazing, as if through a series of framed windows, into the sublime realm of aesthetics—a just reward for the sacrifice.

Even as museums moved into more contemporary structures in the twentieth century, they retained their sober-minded architectural austerity, now presented with a palette of raw concrete and hard-edged minimalism. Galleries—stripped back to nothing more than four white walls—were reserved strictly for encounters with art. These reverential white cubes, so clearly delineated from the museum's social spaces, reinforced the cultural norm of separating art and life—a vestige of sacral architecture in the art museum. When tired, the visitor found few places to rest. Benches were made of hard wood or blocks of stone. Amenities were spartan. The food, served in bright halls reminiscent of high school cafeterias, was forgettable. Any green space around the museum was a pass-through, an afterthought. The message was clear: Culture was meant to be taken seriously; it was all work and no play.

Matters took a turn as art museums gradually shed their rarified air of exclusivity and started measuring their success by the size of their audiences—a development some lamented as a surrender to a commercial logic, but one that did bring more attention to the wants and needs of the public. Correspondingly, museums underwent an architectural costume change as well.

As far back as 1934, the Brooklyn Museum, originally intended to be the largest institution of its kind in the world, made a symbolic decision to remove the grand staircase leading up to the entrance of its imposing neoclassical McKim, Meade & White building. The idea was to make the museum feel more "democratic." Many high-temple museums would follow suit in the decades to come. The politically turbulent 1960s created a new impetus toward cultural democracy, with Paris paving the way. By 1977, the radical, inside-out Centre Georges Pompidou had opened. Conceived by an architectural team led by Renzo Piano and Richard Rogers, it pointedly declared that we no longer needed a boundary between the museum and the street. Twelve years later, I. M. Pei's glass pyramid landed in the courtyard of the Louvre. Like an apparition from both the past and the future, it opened an aperture between the gallery and the gathering space. The museum now not only beckoned everyone. It was an event.

In the latter years of the twentieth century, museum architecture went into overdrive. Aided by advances in building materials, computer-assisted design technologies, and generous public budgets for cultural infrastructure, a period of flamboyant design took hold. It reached its apex in 1997 with Frank Gehry's breathtaking, titanium-clad Guggenheim Bilbao. The structure, designed by an architect who clearly loved art and artists, was justly celebrated and emulated for putting its host city on the map. Yet it was, along with other museums

András Szántó

that followed in a similar vein, a work of art in its own right, outshining its contents, elbowing for attention in the urban landscape as a beacon of globalist ambition. Not since the 1959 opening of Frank Lloyd Wright's building for the Solomon R. Guggenheim Museum in New York, with its bright white, attention-grabbing corkscrew on Fifth Avenue, had people flocked to a museum first and foremost for its architecture.

The formula of commissioning iconic museum buildings from brand-name architects turned out to be a winning one for cities and urban developments in need of cultural anchoring. With China and the Gulf petro-states fueling a museum-building boom in the new millennium, the era of "starchitecture" turned out a series of stunning structures that functioned as both magnets for tourists and emblems of the modernity of their cities and nations.

This expressive approach to museum design, however, has produced mixed results. For all intents and purposes, it substituted one language of authority with another, only marginally less intimidating one. Instead of Corinthian columns, we got shimmering glass. Italian marble gave way to rare metals. Whereas Greek temples and travertine-coated Modernist citadels have come to signify fading cultural hierarchies, these new architectural spectaculars came across in the eyes of many as avatars of the neoliberal order and its stubbornly entrenched chasms of inequity.

Exuberant, supremely confident architecture did help prop up the appeal of museums when other "high" art forms were floundering. But the museum as a work of art was not always kind to works of art themselves. More concerning still, many people came to feel that these alluring structures were not intended for them. Of course, starchitecture was not the only sort of museum design being produced in the 1990s and the early 2000s. Generations of architects had struggled to reconcile the tension between the democratic and the elitist impulses of the art museum. Nonetheless, a realization gradually dawned that the very stratagems intended to lure people into art museums were keeping a substantial portion of the public away.

This anxiety compounded after the 2008 financial crisis, when the post–Cold War status quo came under scrutiny.

A decade later, the reckonings of the pandemic accelerated the shifts in attitude, upending long-held assumptions around museums, including their architecture. Architectural design, like many creative fields, started turning away from the muscular virtuosity of the single venerated visionary—usually male and hailing from the Global North—to more empathetic, collaborative, and distributed forms of creativity that faced toward the public and de-emphasized the author as individual.

Just as a generation of museum leaders began to open the museum up to a larger audience, a generation of architects started to move beyond look-at-me statements and to imagine more welcoming and accessible museums, ones that are intentionally rooted in their communities and urban or natural surroundings. The art of architecture, embracing as it does so many other arts, aligned with new attitudes in the art world. Even architects who had designed their share of iconic museums pivoted toward more restrained and embedded solutions. If there is one message that emanates from the dialogues in this book, it is that the era of museum starchitecture is definitively over.

"The pendulum is swinging," one architect noted during our conversation. "Good architecture does not have to be expensive or superficially spectacular," said another. "I don't really care for the beauty pageant of look-at-me museum design," allowed a third. They all stressed that "we should try to avoid this iconic and monumental architecture" and that "it is no longer enough to produce space just for the sake of awe." The architects expressed disdain for buildings that were "showing off," a mere "attraction," or worse, a "distraction" to paper over the museum's entanglements in the legacies of colonialism and racism.

The architects represented here are looking for "better ways to do architecture," a pivot to "un-monumentality" that emphasizes "human interactions" over shiny structures. "It doesn't mean these weren't absolutely astonishing, memorable buildings," said one of them of the starchitecture period, "but there has been a shift in the last generation."

What these conversations make clear is that museum architecture, no less than the museum itself, is at a pivot point. Architects are realigning intents and methods, building on the

András Szántó

achievements of the past to create inclusive cultural spaces that can meet the moment. In the grand sweep of things, museum architecture is moving away from the design conventions of the museum as a secular church, aiming to convey its relevance in a language that is not so sacral or hierarchical. One way or another, these architects are working to strike a fruitful balance between wonder and humility. They want to create structures that insist on the vitality of the museum as a uniquely necessary civic institution in the service of art and society, while at the same time accommodate all segments of the public.

At its best, this new museum architecture acts as a partner to the emerging twenty-first-century museology.

Remaining Indispensable

What, then, might the future museum be like, not only as an institutional construct, but as a tangible structure and place?

The answer belongs to the twenty-five architects whom I sat with between March and September 2022 to think about the future museum. Eight of them spoke as pairs, reflecting the collaborative nature of architecture. They hail from all around the world, and several operate offices across the globe. With few exceptions, they represent the current middle generation of architects. With the youngest in their early forties and a median age of around fifty, many have years of museum-making ahead of them. Several of them apprenticed with rank-ing members of a prior generation who left an indelible mark on museums. While a few of their names will no doubt be familiar, I felt that it was important to hear from members of the emerging cohort whose outlook on museums is, perhaps, less well known. As with my previous book, I aimed for an even share of female interlocutors, a goal that ran up against the realities of a profession that remains, for the moment, heavily male-dominated at the top.

The dialogues are the result of long conversations and several rounds of collaborative editing in which the original text was abridged and refined to a form that we were all satis-fied with—a process not unlike architecture itself. Each architect was invited to make a sketch capturing the gist of our conversation.

Between them, these architects have been responsible for dozens of art museums, including some of the world's largest and most renowned ones. While they represent a spectrum of viewpoints, the fact that they are all architects working today predisposes them to see the world through certain frames. They are operating in a society dominated by digital culture and the omnipresence of mass media. Their careers have tracked a period of globalization, to which they have contributed symbolically and materially. They are producing architecture for a contemporary art world that has exploded worldwide and blossomed into a polyphonic array of mediums and expressions. They have lived through a period of loosening cultural dualities—between the West and the rest, the Global South and North, male and female, to name some. They belong to the first generation of architects to truly confront a world at the edge of ecological peril.

These architects are not afraid to traverse disciplinary boundaries. Several practice landscape architecture and interior design. Some of them planned to be artists, and quite a few design exhibitions. Their work puts them on the forward edge of thinking about urbanization, transportation, material science, sociology, energy conservation, and global politics. Their connections to the worlds of education, commerce, and entertainment enable them to not only support the project of the future museum, but in certain respects help guide the evolution of the form.

I tried to enter these conversations with no pre-existing hypothesis about what the new museum "hardware" is supposed to look like, feel like, or function like. I am neither an architecture critic nor an historian. I did not set out to write a field guide to today's museum architecture. If anything, I am painfully aware of how many excellent architects and buildings are missing from these pages. I certainly don't intend to propose a unified theory or rule book for museum design. Rather, I approached the task as someone who has advised museums on their strategies and initiatives for some time, trying to understand how we should think about museum buildings in this moment. I viewed the topic through the lenses of a sociologist and a journalist seeking to document the prevailing consensus, if there was one.

András Szántó

And it appears there is. While I am not suggesting these architects think alike, they do align around some fundamentals of museum design. A more or less shared set of convictions crystallized in the conversations, including a passionate belief in the future of the museum as a cultural and architectural typology, and a no less urgent desire for rethinking and renewal.

"To be indispensable," said a designer of many cultural buildings, "the museum cannot be seen as a luxury, but rather as a common necessity." However, "for museums to stay relevant today," this architect added, "they have to embrace autocriticism and irony." "If museum architecture doesn't evolve," another architect warned, "the museum as a social institution will become irrelevant."

Spaces of Encounter

No matter what their individual design approach, the architects I spoke with are determined to break down the museum's conventional formality, hierarchy, and impermeability. They share a remarkably consistent belief in "porous," "transparent," "inclusive," and "open structures"—a "museum without boundaries."

They wish to see "more of a continuum between inside and outside" and to perforate the borders separating the exhibiting and social functions of the museum. They are looking to activate in-between "gray zones," including parks and green spaces, as well as "pocket spaces" inside the buildings, to provide loosely defined, multidimensional spheres of learning, congregation, reflection, and relaxation. They see the museum as a "third space," a site where everyday life happens but that is neither work nor home. They propose a "fluid" architecture that allows art to suffuse the whole museum and life to flow unimpeded through its solemn spaces.

In the eyes of these architects, museums should learn to shape-shift in order to engage a culture in perpetual flux. They must be able to mutate "from one shape to another," moving past "the idea that a museum is a monofunctional building." Echoing recent shifts in museological thinking, the architects imagine the museum as a performative space where the visitors—the actors on the stage, so to speak—are empowered to take control of the narrative. Several spoke of handing over more "agency" to visitors, releasing them from heavy curatorial intermediation so they can become "active participants" in the museum experience, charting their own journeys through the building and selecting objects at whim. "Flexibility" may be the word I heard most often during my months of conversations.

When asked to define the museum itself, the architects echoed the sentiments of the museum directors in *The Future of the Museum*. They spoke of it as a "cultural community center of any agglomeration of human beings—their forum, their reception room, and their public room"; as a "place where difficult societal conversations can be held in the widest space possible"; as a "wake-up call that pulls you out of all those distractions and into the present"; as an "escape out of the real world"; as a "place of freedom where one can question society, reinvent, innovate"; as an institution where "everyone can be comfortable by themselves and express themselves creatively, while being kind to each other."

These architects see museums as "spaces of encounter" that are devoted to sharing knowledge, "very intimate" while also "serious fun." They describe the museum as a "truly civic space," a piece of "cultural and communal infrastructure" that engages people with art and ideas, yet also allows them every now and then to "slow down and focus" and opt out of the relentless "distraction and fast pace" of modern life.

In this kind of museum, "everything is sensitized, visually and aurally." Enhanced experience, however, is not achieved through an "austerity and neutrality of the spaces." The white-walled gallery, a legacy of the mid-twentieth century, is not the answer. "Exhibiting art does not necessitate white cubes," noted one of my conversation partners, articulating a surprisingly common view. It is "too pristine," too controlled and confining. The whole museum experience "could be decentralized," not just within the individual museum building, but in relation to the community, with the museum projecting itself outward "with satellites across the entire city."

The architects I spoke with know that we are in the midst of a transitional phase for museums, when institutions of all kinds are widely questioned. They are mindful that museums must

　　　　　　　　　　　　　　András Szántó

align with the current "historical moment of revision of the Western narrative and the colonial narrative"—a generational shift with profound consequences for both the software and the hardware of the institution.

They recognize, too, that museums, as civic structures, must be part of the vanguard of climate action. The entire sector needs to be future-proofed. Taken to heart, climate awareness involves tamping down museums' seemingly insatiable appetite for new construction. "Putting up a building is not the way forward," one of them declared. "We need to remember our position in nature," pleaded a designer of structures made from locally sourced materials. Several architects spoke of drawing inspiration from ancestral building technologies. Solutions are hiding in plain sight. "Let's look at how humanity has adapted and survived, and let's learn from our biological and ecological histories," suggested an architect who has studied impoverished communities in West Africa. A generation's priorities are revealed in the words of the architect who said, "We need to think of the architecture of the future always in relation to nature."

One vexing realization for many of these architects is that permanent structures may not make sense in an unstable future world. Cultural entities will need to "outlast their current functions." We cannot know what kind of museum will fit the future. Already, startlingly original concepts pop up in these dialogues, from buildings that can customize spaces in real time to adapt to artworks; to museums in which living rural customs, such as tofu-making, become the exhibited content; to cultural spaces harmonized with natural sites, including caves; to digitally outfitted structures in which the entire museum can be changed at the flip of a switch with a remote system update.

Today's architects are certainly being drawn into a conversation about what a museum will look like in a fully digital society. "All institutions are contending with the repercussions of the internet age," said one, "which has completely challenged the singularity of authority, and correspondingly forced architecture to rethink how the stage is set for a believable engagement between experts and citizens."

Will a future in which digital artifacts predominate even allow for, let alone demand, physical places to assemble and display physical objects? How far will tomorrow's digital museums deviate from today's physical ones?

Several architects in this book have been commissioned to design for the metaverse. But few of them think digital architecture will abandon the spatial typologies of real-world museums anytime soon. "I believe in physical connections, in the feelings of physical dimensions, and gravity as well," said one. Most insist on the enduring, perhaps even growing appeal of analog spaces, to satisfy our "yearning for the patina of the real" amidst a life of gazing at screens. There are hardwired limits to how far you can push the limits of digital design: "Take too great a leap," said another, "and you might simply lose the audience."

Despite the formidable uncertainties confronting the museum, the architects are sanguine about its prospects—so long as it can adapt. They believe architecture can be a catalyst in this transformation. "We can make sure that museums are pioneers, part of the avant-garde," said one. "Not just the artistic avant-garde, but the social avant-garde."

Touchstones

I wrote my last book at the height of a pandemic. I never imagined I would write this one in a time of war. Unease about the sacking of Ukraine, along with a panoply of other crises—from the lingering toll of Covid-19 to chronic economic disparities and ideological polarization to the indisputable portents of climate breakdown—loomed large behind all of these conversations. On the bright side, the tribulations of the hour provide an impetus for new thinking. "Now, between Covid and the war in Ukraine," proposed an architect who has been making museums for decades, "we can ask more fundamental questions."

Of course, museum architects have been asking fundamental questions for some time, and they have responded with buildings that serve as touchstones for today's practitioners. The pantheon of referential museums mentioned in the course of my conversations, by no means exhaustive, includes classic museums, such as Karl Friedrich Schinkel's Altes Museum and Mies van der Rohe's Neue Nationalgalerie, both in Berlin. The midcentury icons ranged from Wright's New York Guggenheim to the spellbinding statements of Latin American Modernism, especially

András Szántó

Oscar Niemeyer's canopy for Ibirapuera Park, in São Paulo; Affonso Eduardo Reidy's Museum of Modern Art in Rio de Janeiro; and Mexico's City's National Museum of Anthropology, with its monumental concrete umbrella providing shade for a courtyard set around a man-made pond, by Pedro Ramírez Vázquez, Jorge Campuzano, and Rafael Mijares Alcérreca.

Among the more recent projects singled out as inspirations for today's working architects were Herzog & de Meuron's immense Turbine Hall for the Tate Modern in London; the Austrian architect Hans Hollein's postmodern designs for Frankfurt and Mönchengladbach; Rafael Moneo's Fundació Pilar i Joan Miró in Palma de Mallorca, Spain; Tadao Ando's compositions in light and concrete, culminating in his sublime complex of museums in Naoshima, Japan; the Swiss minimalist Peter Zumthor's Kunsthaus Bregenz in Austria; Teodoro González de León and Abraham Zabludovsky's Museo Tamayo in Mexico City; the Louvre Abu Dhabi, among the most poetic of Jean Nouvel's many museums; Paulo Mendes da Rocha's Brazilian Museum of Sculpture in São Paulo; the Japanese architectural firm SANAA's translucent structures, most notably the 21st Century Museum of Contemporary Art Kanazawa; Frank Gehry's aforementioned works in Bilbao and beyond; Lacaton & Vassal's gritty, bare-boned renovation of the Palais de Tokyo in Paris; Rem Koolhaas's open-ended Kunsthal Rotterdam and his firm's buildings for the urban campus of the Garage Museum of Contemporary Art in Moscow; and Renzo Piano's seminal contributions to museum architecture, including the Fondation Beyeler in Basel, with its intimate scale and connection to the neighboring fields and gardens.

Countless other precedents, too many to name here, inform and inspire the work of today's museum architects. But three turned up repeatedly in the conversations. Together, this trio describes a space of imagination and possibility that already decades ago gestured toward the future museum.

The Centre Georges Pompidou, in Paris, arguably the most iconic museum building of them all, opened a generation's eyes to the cultural, spatial, and urbanistic potential of the museum, with its transparent walls, column-free spaces, and guts revealed in vivid primary colors. "It has this wonderful porosity," noted an architect who lives and works nearby. "It is connected to the city, constantly active through the plaza in the front, and by virtue of how the space inside can be used in a flexible way."

Like the Centre Pompidou, Lina Bo Bardi's Brutalist structure for the Museu de Arte de São Paulo, known as MASP, which opened in 1968, is distinguished by a public space attached to the museum that is given over to the pulsing energy of the city. Exhibition spaces were pushed upward and downward, leaving a vast plaza—the largest covered span in Latin America at the time—that one architect described as "a place of reunion, celebration, protest, and representation, where everything happens."

The most frequently cited inspiration in these dialogues was the Louisiana Museum of Modern Art, which sits on a gorgeous coastal promontory a short drive north of Copenhagen. Established in 1958 with three Scandinavian Modern buildings designed by Vilhelm Wohlert and Jørgen Bo, the museum consists of simple structures connected by glass corridors that contribute to a seamless fusion of art, architecture, and nature. An architect born nearby described its "sense of timelessness" as being rooted in a "constant exploration of the relationship between inside and outside."

These three often-cited predecessors demonstrate that there is continuity in the aspirations of museum architecture. They presage many of the qualities that today's architects expect to find in tomorrow's museums. They are experiments in "desacralizing" the museum, in demonstrating that institutions can "unlearn hierarchy and control" and "get closer to everyday life." They attempt to offer a "sense of welcome and empathy" that is "more participatory" and "less institutional." They open up a "landscape of opportunities and activities."

A Step Forward

To avoid any misunderstanding, none of the architects in this book is suggesting the museum should become some kind of anodyne community space. No one is proposing to kick the objects to the corner and abandon the museum's edifying and research functions, turning it into funhouse entertainment. A great deal about the future museum will remain constant out of necessity. "A room full of paintings from the Dutch Golden

András Szántó

Age or French Impressionists is unlikely to change much," said one architect. "You will always need walls to hang them on, and spaces of contemplation in which you can admire them." The museum, as the pinnacle of civic architecture, should continue to surprise, delight, and comfort future visitors.

What the architects in this volume—along with the directors in *The Future of the Museum*—do espouse is an upgrade, a step forward. They seek to deliver the expert knowledge and meaningful experiences museums uniquely provide, but also to remove visible and invisible barriers to entry, to bring these cherished institutions more into sync with life as it is lived now.

At the core of this line of thinking is a simple notion: that the museum belongs to all of us. While I was working on my last book, ICOM, the global federation of museums, was attempting to formulate a new definition of the museum. A December 2019 proposal had failed. Then, as this book neared completion, in late summer 2022, ICOM delegates met again. This time a new definition received resounding approval:

> *A museum is a not-for-profit, permanent institution in the service of society that researches, collects, conserves, interprets and exhibits tangible and intangible heritage. Open to the public, accessible and inclusive, museums foster diversity and sustainability. They operate and communicate ethically, professionally and with the participation of communities, offering varied experiences for education, enjoyment, reflection and knowledge sharing.*

The key phrase here is *in the service of society*. A museum should benefit everyone, even in today's polarized public life. Such a simple idea might arouse skepticism. Conservatives might assail it for being woke. Progressives may find it doesn't reach far enough. Yet one can only hope that there is a space—in the abstract and the physical senses of the word—for people of all beliefs and from all walks of life to come together.

What I am referring to is what used to be called, plain and simple, "public space." Or what the nineteenth-century American landscape designer Frederick Law Olmsted called the sphere of "commonplace civilization"—a domain of shared experience, like Olmsted's magnificent parks, that all people could access and enjoy. It's no coincidence that so many architects bring up parks and libraries—two low-threshold spaces that are, crucially, free to enter in most cities—as models for tomorrow's art institutions. Generations of thinkers have put forward similar ideas about the underpinnings of a healthy, open society that can offer an antidote to the atomizing tendencies of modern life. At their best, museums can provide precisely such a sense of belonging.

I began by saying that this book is about a search for new museum hardware that can match the new museology captured in my earlier conversations with institutional leaders. The architects all conveyed a similar sense of urgency about the need for recalibration. The tumultuous experience of our recent past has accelerated a transition from the museum as a temple on a hill to a more engaged and democratic institution.

Architects are tasked with translating these evolving ideals into tangible, functional, practical forms. But architecture alone—contending as it must with legacy structures, demanding clients, and the physical constraints of sites and materials—cannot coax out the full capacities of institutions. And a museum should never be confused with its building—it is so much more. What architecture can do is help museums get closer to achieving their potential.

We thus come full circle, back to the software coursing through these buildings. The truth of the matter is that a great museum can function in a mediocre building, but no amount of architecture will make a great museum out of one lacking strong art or a thoughtful program. Adapting to an ever-changing society, the museum building, like the museum itself, will always remain in a state of construction. If architecture can be a partner and guide on this journey, it will have served its purpose well.

András Szántó

The Dialogues

KULAPAT YANTRASAST
WHY Architecture, Los Angeles & New York City

A VISIT TO A MUSEUM SHOULD BE LIKE ENJOYING A GARDEN OF IDEAS AND STORIES

In the summer of 2022, I met up with Kulapat Yantrasast, founder of the Los Angeles–based architecture firm WHY, for steamed dumplings on a balcony overlooking the circular courtyard of Art Basel, in Switzerland. Wearing his trademark bright-colored jumpsuit, the architect greeted passing acquaintances every few seconds, it seemed. Cheerful and energetic, Yantrasast, who is in his early fifties, is a ubiquitous presence on the global art scene. His biography predisposes him to be the epitome of the twenty-first-century culturally multi-lingual, peripatetic architect: a youth spent in Thailand; early career in Japan, working alongside Tadao Ando, minimalist master of concrete and light; eventually founding his own studio in California, the seat of today's and tomorrow's cultural industries. Yantrasast's practice extends beyond architecture to landscape design, furniture making, cuisine, and other creative pursuits. Uniting his museum projects is a belief in human-centered buildings that are open and accessible to all.

ANDRÁS SZÁNTÓ *I recently had the pleasure of walking through your extension for the Asian Art Museum in San Francisco, as well as your galleries in the Academy Museum of Motion Pictures Arts and Sciences, in Los Angeles. What guides your thinking about museums?*

KULAPAT YANTRASAST Museums, with their Western origins, are sites of presentation and exclusivity. They were driven by class identities and exhibiting rare possessions. Museums consequentially symbolized a singular culture with a capital *C*. Architecturally, then, most historic museums were built as temples—for cults more than cultures. But this obsolete notion of the museum as a temple is on its way out. What we need now is a new and inclusive cultural platform.

Working in various places in America, I was shocked and angry to learn that many people were historically barred from going inside museums. The path toward becoming a relevant place for cultures in the twenty-first century demands a full acknowledgment of the lessons of the past and a radical inclusivity that is open to all people. This must be achieved in both the hardware and the software of the museum, architecturally and programmatically.

We definitely seem to be in a critical moment in the history of the museum.

The awakening of the museum from the software perspective has been clear. The decolonizing of the museum, equality, and inclusivity are among the most critical issues of our times. Yet when it comes to museum architecture and design, these subjects are still not being addressed head-on. If museum architecture doesn't evolve, the museum as a social institution will become irrelevant. It will not fit the new programs that societies need in order for us to grow and thrive as a whole.

You once described your practice as architecture that makes people like each other. Where does that aspiration come from?

I was born in Bangkok, Thailand. My parents are Chinese and Thai; I am a cultural mutt. Bangkok has a radical, inclusive social fluidity. Everyone looks out for one another in an intrinsic connectivity, almost like an ecology of plants. I then went

Kulapat Yantrasast

to study in Japan and lived there for fifteen years, eight of them spent working closely with Tadao Ando, my mentor. But despite my deep love of refined Japanese cultures, I came to feel that as we keep abstracting architecture, we miss some essences of real living, of that diverse mash-up or spontaneous improvisation—a vibrant sense of being human. I felt the need to combine my Thai and Japanese roots, and figured America would be a good ground for exploration. Here, I hope to develop a clear yet complex architectural language while incorporating other voices, disparate interests, and even conflicting agendas into one shared architecture.

In which of your museums do you feel you have accomplished that goal?

The Grand Rapids Art Museum, built in 2007 in Michigan, the first art museum in the world to receive LEED Gold certification for environmental sustainability, is a good case study. Its goal is to balance an inspiring art experience with full commitments to its communities and environments. It serves as a sanctuary of cultures, and a welcoming portico and living room of the city. For the design of the American Museum of Natural History's Northwest Coast Hall, I personally spent a few months living, and years conversing, with the nations and communities along the coast. We include countless voices from the people whose artworks are highlighted. Yes, the museum presents art objects, but it is fundamentally about the people, their human stories, their creative lives behind the objects.

This, in a nutshell, is where the museum is headed—a place of social encounters as much as a storehouse for treasures. How might you achieve that at The Met, where you are currently transforming a suite of galleries?

Our team is responsible for redesigning The Met's Rockefeller Wing, which houses the arts of Africa, Oceania, and the Americas. The goal is to provide an uplifting destination for art and also a special place for people. Previously, artworks from three-quarters of the world got squished up into one wing, and these regions have so little in common. Critically, the design needs to bring recognition to the different cultures and clarity to the creative roots and contemporary societies. The gallery is designed for people to feel at ease, ready for their own discoveries. There are places to sit, contemplate, and even relax with Central Park. The planning takes advantage of sightlines and natural light—you might be a hundred feet from the window, but you'll still have glimpses of the light and the park outside.

I want to dig into design solutions that help to realize this idea of empathy. You mentioned the portico, the idea of in-between spaces, fuzzy perimeters. What else is there?

Many people perceive museum design merely as form-making, that an art museum should look like a sculpture. I don't think architecture should try to mimic sculpture. The potentials of architecture lie in the spaces, experiences, and meaningful interactions it can host and empower for people engaging with multiple art forms.

When visiting museums, I often ask myself, "When and why do I feel connected and inspired?" In *The Image of the City*, a book published in 1960, Kevin Lynch, a godfather of urban planning, talks about what makes a city memorable. It's about clarity of circulation and districts, recognition of landmarks and nodes. Museum design might offer a similar image for visitors' experiences. Architecturally, the building should have high artistic qualities and civic presence. Experientially, it should provide spaces that encourage people to wander and make their own journeys. A visit to the museum should be like enjoying a garden of ideas and stories; there is no right or wrong way to visit a garden. You should build your own narrative and explore what your experience might be.

The possibilities for people to find new stories and ideas are essential. People should own their experiences, rather than being told what to see or do. Having places for people to sit down, ponder, or daydream is key. Many new museums are planned mainly to cope with the large mass of visitors, so the circulation becomes like a conveying system. Visitors move from one painting to another, in a row, back to back. There is no place to slow down and look closely. It is crucial to provide "pocket spaces" in between artworks, so people can think about what they are experiencing and be in the moment.

Kulapat Yantrasast

I like the term "pocket spaces"—these oases of sociability. But you can also go the other way, injecting exhibition elements into what were formerly considered non-art spaces. These two zones of the museum are often kept separate.

Museums' rigid separation between gallery and non-gallery spaces is being reconsidered, just as the sacred and the profane are being reconfigured in temples and plazas. The solution is not to mix everything up completely, but rather to insert things in between. And at the right moments, it's also adding pocket spaces of sitting areas for discussion between groups of gallery spaces, or presenting art moments in between public or educational spaces. Museums do have these components in their programs, but the strategic planning and distribution of mixed integration have not been creatively explored.

Which institutions have succeeded in creating this sense of welcome and interwovenness, in your eyes?

The Louisiana Museum of Modern Art in Denmark is a great example for integrating nature, activities, and contemplative art experiences; it is lively and uplifting. The Menil Collection, in Houston, shows us a way in which museums could fuse into the community, weaving everyday life with inspiring moments that art provides. The WHY-designed Institute of Contemporary Art in Los Angeles is a good study of a full mash-up where galleries, museum offices, art classrooms, visitors' lounges, and a library are interwoven in overlapping spaces, right in the heart of downtown.

To your point about humility, many feel that we are in a post–Guggenheim Bilbao moment, a post-look-at-me moment. Many people seem to be skeptical about architecture that makes grand statements.

The previous generation was about "great patron and architect know best." Patron and architect were often working as one, two experts making a private cultural project that would become public later. Of course, some museums made that way worked well. But many others failed.

However, cultures today are not necessarily made by elite and exclusive select fews anymore. Architecturally, what's important for our generation is not just changing the style of building, making it more modern and open, with more glass, or adding new components to the museum, like co-working or cafés. This new beginning is fundamentally about democratizing the process of making the museum. You start by engaging and empowering the people whose cultures are present and whose voices are central, rather than assuming what cultural programs and representations they need.

Is it also more about urbanism than "just" architecture?
That's one aspect of it. When it comes to the museum of the future, I think it should be a hybrid of social and cultural touchpoints. It should synergize with other social entities—with a school, a hotel, a workspace, or even collective or senior housing. Conceptually and experientially, we need to bring more ideas and discussions to the table. How could these touchpoints be planned and activated? Cultural clubs or third places, like Soho House, are trying to do something similar. They are making cultural hubs via hospitality, co-working, and social networking. The museum would benefit from looking into such hybrid approaches.

There is, of course, a hybrid of a museum and a hotel, the Benesse House in Naoshima, Japan, by your mentor Tadao Ando. Your own practice expands even wider, to include food, garden design, and what you call "human flourishing." Is that part of a generational attitude?
My approach is in some ways a reaction to the previous generation, where *The Fountainhead* was the ideal—this obsession with the lone-wolf genius. I think our generation needs to focus on developing a great, inclusive orchestra, rather than celebrating an elite prima donna. We need to work hard to forge clear, strong, and comprehensive solutions. What I could start is a personal mash-up of what I love in Japan and Thailand. While I appreciate the abstraction and refinement of Japanese architecture and crafts, I also have a deep love for the warm, colorful, and messy jives, and the open-ended improvisation, in Thai creative forms.

Kulapat Yantrasast

What do Los Angeles and the West Coast, where you live, mean to you?

I feel like I have become an unofficial ambassador of Los Angeles. Of all big cities in the world, L.A. is one of the very few whose main industries are creative. We are not a banking, farming, or logistics city; we thrive on creative industries—films, music, advertising, design, architecture, and many more. People in L.A. are curious about what's going on in cultures and trends; they want to connect and engage. In that sense, L.A. has one of the best infrastructures for cultural production and distribution. In L.A., you feel a sense of freedom and a welcoming vibe of come-as-you-are. The city leaves you alone; you can experiment and make mistakes. You have space to invent.

With all of that in mind, then, how would you define a museum?

It's funny, everyone keeps trying to find another word: an art center, a *mediathèque*, a *kunsthalle*, an art institute. *Museum* seems like such a loaded term now. I struggle with its connotations, too. I want to see the museum defined as a vibrant cultural touchpoint that allows us to engage with diverse histories and other people's ideas and stories. In addition, I go to museums when I want space of my own or time to think—so it is also a crucial touchpoint with myself. I go to museums for different reasons at different times: to ponder and try to understand, to look at something in particular, to get inspiration. These multiple aspects of a museum visit help me experience art and cultures and the world, as well as explore my own thought process and creative approach.

I'm glad you brought up multiple visitor motivations. Previously museums were by and large designed through a single, expert curatorial filter. How can you design for multidimensionality, to accommodate these varied motivations?

The museum is moving from a lone voice to multiple voices. At work, I often say diversity starts in the kitchen, from the get-go. We need different voices, disparate perspectives, and communication tools for us to connect and adapt. For architects, it is crucial to be open-minded and to help stakeholders and communities visualize ideas or design options, so we can make a collective decision together. Spatially, nimbleness and flexibility are much needed. The hardware needs to be open for future software upgrades for the museum to operate.

Richard Rogers spoke about "loose fit" spaces, and the Centre Pompidou, which he designed with Renzo Piano, tried to allow for this looseness, accepting that cultural needs will change in the future.

Centre Pompidou and MASP in São Paulo, by Lina Bo Bardi, share a similar spirit. They are superstructures that deploy innovative structural engineering to house large, column-free spaces where many activities could flexibly happen. But with flexibility, scale and proportion play critical roles. At the Pompidou, the exhibition space is so vast that gallery boxes had to be inserted inside for art installations, which are similar to convention centers or art fairs. Flexibility alone is not enough. It needs to be counterbalanced with space design that makes people feel engaged and encouraged.

What are some things that frustrate you about the museums you visit?

I don't really care for the beauty pageant of look-at-me museum design. One can't help but admire some museums that were built as temples, holding the light for art with a capital *A*. The Kimbell Art Museum, in Fort Worth, Texas, is a great example. It is beloved by architects, myself included. But it is celebrated in the age-old sense of the art temple, timeless and spiritual. We also need fresh museums for the twenty-first century, museums that serve as contemporary cultural intersections. It frustrates me when museum architecture focuses only on its own endorsement and isn't intended to shelter and empower other arts and cultural activities.

What else must you incorporate to remain relevant tomorrow?

I would highlight two considerations among many: enhanced physical experiences and inventive programming. By physical experiences I mean beauty, comfort, and an uplifting spirit. These need to be integrated with digital technologies, augmented or virtual realities. Inventive programs, meanwhile,

Kulapat Yantrasast

should expand and redefine how museums matter to the public. Museum professionals are working on new ways to engage diverse audiences. From the architect's point of view, interconnectivity and interweaving are key. In addition to the cultural content, the museum experience is absolutely about people. Museums are social experiences. They are about civic pride and empathy-building. We must not forget this.

Can empathy-building be achieved in the digital realm? Experiments with digital museums tend to look like fake modern concrete palaces, for now.
We are only at the first step of integrating and transfusing the new virtual into the physical world, so things are not fully formed. But humans are nimble and open to change. New technologies force us to adapt, but they also force us to evolve.

When that happens, we may feel nostalgic for those well-established norms of spatial experience in museums. So how might you imagine the visitor journey in the future?
Museum experiences will become so rich and diverse in the future. The museum as a temple, that quality of timelessness and spirituality, would still exist. It might be more cherished, as people in the digital age seek something real to hold on to. Expanding beyond that role, museums will function as cultural hubs and civic sites to connect people, share stories, program communal activities, and forge mutual understanding. The museum has endless potentials to empower dialogues and cultural interactions.

What is the design process that gets you to your kind of museum?
Active listening and radical engaging are underrated skills for architects. You have to function as a sociologist who cares about the communities you are building for. Our job is to present every creative possibility we can imagine for those communities to experience and explore. "Think global, act local" is still a valid motto. Sometimes you have to show communities other successful museums around the world, so they can imagine, together with you, the future we want and ought to build.

I would like to finish on how architects should approach their work, today and tomorrow. We're living in a time of chronic divisions, tensions, crises. How do you see your contribution, as a creator of places that are meant to be shared emblems of communities?

The architect shouldn't be a prima donna. The job we are tasked with in this contested time is that of an emphatic conductor, not a diva. As a conductor you celebrate each and every voice in the orchestra, and you define the rules of successful engagement. Smart complexity requires the disparate parts to engage well and synergize together. If one listens, observes, and tries to understand the communities, and if one is willing to weave all the voices into a mix and build an inclusive solution to house all that complexity, then the museum can be the key to empathy and even "world peace," for sure.

Kulapat Yantrasast

PAULA ZASNICOFF CARDOSO
& CARLOS ALBERTO MACIEL
Arquitetos Associados, Belo Horizonte, Brazil

AN OASIS CAN SAVE YOUR LIFE

Like any design enthusiast, when I visited Brazil
I marveled at the boldness and profusion of the
country's extraordinary Modernist architecture. Few
museums have been as influential for their design
as the Museu de Arte de São Paulo (MASP). Its 1968
Brutalist glass-and-concrete structure by Lina Bo Bardi
elevated the galleries above street level, allowing
everyday life to flow unimpeded below the institution
and influencing generations of socially minded architects. Among those are the members of Arquitetos
Associados, a collaborative practice dedicated to architecture and urban design. The partners, including Paula
Zasnicoff Cardoso and Carlos Alberto Maciel, have
designed some of Brazil's most celebrated visual-arts
buildings, including several at Instituto Inhotim, the
vast indoor-outdoor arts complex situated not far from
the architects' home base of Belo Horizonte, in south-
eastern Brazil. Currently at work on an addition to São
Paulo's Pinacoteca art museum, Cardoso and Maciel
believe in museum architecture that can blend seamlessly with both natural and social environments.

an oasis can save your life

MM: Canal

2022

ANDRÁS SZÁNTÓ *You are Brazilian architects working in a land of extraordinary architecture, the country of Lina Bo Bardi and Oscar Niemeyer. What does this mean for your practice?*

PAULA ZASNICOFF CARDOSO A lot. We are part of Arquitetos Associados, a collaborative studio founded with three other partners (Alexandre Brasil, André Luiz Prado, and Bruno Santa Cecília) and dedicated to architecture and urbanism. Each project is developed as a unique and specific work. We have different points of view, but we always depart from shared premises. Brazilian Modernism is certainly a point of departure, with all of its contradictions and marvelous solutions.

Is there such a thing as a Latin American perspective on museum architecture? And if so, what would it be?

CARLOS ALBERTO MACIEL I don't know if there is a Latin American perspective. But there is a broader way of looking at architecture, including museum architecture, which is connected to climate. The modern period in Brazil coincided with the moment when Brazil became an urban country. One attribute of the new museums built at that time was integration with the landscape to form a kind of continuity between different domains. An example is the park for the Museum of Modern Art in Rio de Janeiro, by Affonso Eduardo Reidy, a Brutalist structure with façades that are completely integrated into the landscape of the ocean and the land. In São Paulo, the MASP building is another example, with its integration into the urban domain, the street, with that continuous platform under the building, an important public space for the city of São Paulo. The canopy Oscar Niemeyer built for the Ibirapuera Park in São Paulo, which eventually housed a museum of modern art, is another example. Some of this is specifically Brazilian. We can have open buildings because our climate allows this kind of openness and continuity.

These ideas about integration with nature and public space are, of course, at the cutting edge of today's thinking about museums. In Brazil, you have a head start. Your practice has designed several private art galleries, major buildings for Inhotim, and now an addition to São Paulo's Pinacoteca. Can you sum up your approach to designing art-museum buildings?

PZC We are living in a historical moment of revision of the Western narrative and the colonial narrative, which includes making room for communities that were historically silenced— women, Indigenous peoples, minorities. In parallel, we are experiencing political polarization, the environmental crisis, increasing inequality, and extreme conservative governments coming to power. I want to believe that our current harsh reality is the last breath of this oppressive worldview. In this context, art museums are moving toward the inclusion of minority narratives. This is a promising path, but an arduous one. Museums should always welcome diversity, uncertainties, and even conflicts.

CAM Central to our discussions about these spaces is how they relate to the landscape and to the exterior world. We emphasize transitions, integrations, and alterations between exterior and interior as a way of relaxing a segregation between the white, controlled, abstract space of the art gallery and the exuberant, natural surrounding domain.

I like to say the white cube is a period room, something we carry with us from the mid-twentieth century. It is an inheritance from the past.

PZC We took part in an exhibition in Pittsburgh curated by Raymund Ryan, who produced a book in 2012 titled *White Cube, Green Maze: New Art Landscapes* that explored this issue. We definitely agree that the white cube is about the past. I don't think the green maze is the only answer. But we are moving toward a design approach related to communities and speci- ficities connected to where the museums are being implanted. The context has to be the point of departure.

You are both immersed in architectural theory, and here I am reminded of the painter Barnett Newman's dictum, "Aesthetics is to art what ornithology is to birds." Still, I wonder: Which ideas from the discourse around architecture have you found to be helpful in thinking about new museum typologies?

CAM I can think of three aspects, which are linked to different authors and theories. First, tectonics: how buildings can reveal their potential in the way they are built. A second is flexibility: how the building can be defined not in functional terms, but via its indeterminacy—as architecture's response to an unpredictable world. And third, the urban condition: how buildings should be considered part of a larger system, the city. These aspects together provide an approximation of how we think about the museum in theoretical terms.

PZC I thought Carlos would mention Henri Lefebvre, the French philosopher and sociologist, and his 1973 writing, later published as a book, *Towards an Architecture of Enjoyment*, which talks about the origins of architecture as coercive and repressive, like a fortress—basically, how buildings were historically used to repress people. We are going in the other direction. We pursue what we call "the disappearance of architecture," which involves eliminating limiting and constraining elements and using materials and techniques that take into account local specificities and environmental concerns.

Let's be more literal. Which museum buildings do you admire the most?

PZC Carlos has already named the two I would mention: MASP from Lina Bo Bardi and Affonso Eduardo Reidy's MAM. The refurbishment of the São Paulo Pinacoteca by Paulo Mendes da Rocha undoubtedly inspires us, and especially the new building we are developing for that institution. Internationally, I would mention the 21st Century Museum of Contemporary Art, in Kanazawa, Japan, by SANAA, where the galleries and programmatic functions are organized in a circular form—a metaphor of a city—with a glass perimeter that dematerializes the edges of the museum.

CAM I would add the Fundació Pilar i Joan Miró in Palma de Mallorca, Spain, by Rafael Moneo. It is a very introspective space, with a potent materiality and a remarkable control of light through translucent alabaster panels, as in his cathedral for Los Angeles. It provides a powerful experience in a surprising and unexpected location.

Given all that, how do you define a museum?

CAM It is more than a building, first of all. This is a specific answer for a Brazilian architect, because we have a tradition of building museums without institutions. Politicians around the country used to hire mainly Oscar Niemeyer to build museums that were not culturally anchored in their communities. Now we are seeing an effort being made to build significant collections and create a kind of relevance for these museums. Museums are complex buildings, architecturally speaking. They demand highly controlled spaces to exhibit and conserve collections, but at the same time they desire to be open, generous, and inviting.

PZC For me, museums create connections and enlarge points of view. They have recently become increasingly democratic and open. In addition to collecting, conserving, educating, and providing access to art, they expand meanings and relationships between art and people. The Brazilian critic Mário Pedrosa used the metaphor of an elastic glove that can adapt to the hands of a free creator. I guess this is a good metaphor to use in relation to museums and how they should relate to culture and communities.

Yet all too often, that glove doesn't fit. Society is changing fast—and not always in a good way. To adapt, what does museum architecture need to unlearn and do differently?

CAM It needs to unlearn hierarchy and control. It needs to get closer to everyday life.

PZC It needs to be open to conflict. And it needs to listen to all voices.

Let's zoom ahead. How, ultimately, will tomorrow's museums look and feel different? What will surprise us about them?

PZC We may be surprised to find that they look to the past. They might be more connected with context and community issues. They could valorize the specificity of the local context, what some now call "ancestrality." Maybe looking to the future also means staring into the past.

As you noted, museums are becoming more grounded in community, more socially engaged. That's the new software. How can this aspiration be translated into stone and glass and wood?

PZC The Brazilian historian, professor, and artist Flávio Motta coined the term *significant unnamed spaces*, which are beyond the programmatic functions of the museum. Brazilian modern architecture has produced many such undefined spaces, including the plaza under MASP and the Niemeyer canopy. These spaces have a great architectural quality but no functional determination. I think this unnamed space will be more and more connected with museums.

CAM This relates to the reduction of control and hierarchy and what museums should unlearn and learn. We architects need to learn how to improve friendly connections, how to open doors. We recently redesigned the entrance halls of the Pinacoteca. The first action was to open up the doors. There are some subtle aspects in this design strategy concerning hierarchy and control that can be proven to invite people in.

PZC A sense of welcome—an open-door strategy.

That door inevitably opens to politics. Brazil is a complicated country. Paula already said the museum should be open to conflict. But some say the museum should stand apart, as a kind of oasis, a refuge from everyday life. That's another contradiction to navigate.

PZC I agree that a museum should also be an oasis, along with being a place to accommodate all visions, to have wider visions of the world. That's why I said it should accommodate conflict. That is exactly what we are trying to develop in these unnamed spaces, which can accommodate both marvels and conflicts—as urban space does.

CAM There is another way to consider the oasis. An oasis can save your life. The museum is a space where debate can happen in a profound way. It can enable discussions as a way of saving lives, because you have the best opportunity to educate yourself there—not to be educated, but to educate yourself.

This is backdrop, I believe, for why you call the museum a free-dom platform. Can you elaborate on what you mean by that?
PZC This idea of not being educated but educating yourself relates to the disappearance of architecture. I remember the passage from one of Bo Bardi's books when she recounts when John Cage was visiting São Paulo. They passed by MASP, and Cage asked to stop the car. He ran up to the building and said, "This is the architecture of freedom." Lina would say that when she developed that space, she was thinking about how that space should be nothing. This seventy-meter span, the longest in Latin America for many years, was intended to accommodate nothing—and therefore everything. This illustrates beautifully what we mean by the idea of the freedom platform.
CAM If I had to describe it in architectural terms, it is a space that is sufficiently equipped, but also sufficiently indeterminate in functional terms, that it can allow or stimulate unexpected actions and events. This comes from our understanding of architecture as part infrastructure and part event. Time is important because it builds meaning that is not predetermined. That's maybe what Lina meant by saying the space under MASP is about nothing—nothing in functional terms, but also in terms of its meaning. It is unnamed.

I understand your notion of architectural space as a blank can-vas, waiting to be defined by those who use it. But when I hear the word freedom, *I wonder, freedom for whom? And from what? This is an ideological proposition.*
CAM Yes, in a sense. When rethinking the idea of museums specifically, it is exactly an attempt to reduce, as Paula says, the restrictions or the coercive aspect of that architecture. It is a cry for public spaces instead of private spaces. It is an attempt to improve congregation instead of segregation.
PZC It is also about equality, giving access and proper condi-tions to accommodate everyone in a very unequal society.
CAM There is another aspect of freedom nestled in the idea about the museum being a place where people can educate themselves. You deconstruct hierarchy through knowledge. It is a kind of reduction of dominance.

Paula Zasnicoff Cardoso & Carlos Alberto Maciel

Practically speaking, when do you feel you have succeeded in realizing this freedom platform as a mode of architecture? What, in other words, is the architectural language of the freedom platform?

CAM One example is the Burle Marx Education Center in Inhotim, designed by Paula and Alexandre Brasil, which was the first large building our office did there. In contrast to typical museums, which are very closed, it was a fully open space, designed to receive students and visitors. It has two domains: a shade behind the slab, and the sunny space over the slab that is a water garden. What you get is a kind of relaxed mediation between interior and exterior, where you cannot say exactly whether you are inside or outside. The landscape of the garden is mixed with the landscape of the building.

Freedom is not only about structures, but also about atmosphere. The ambience of museums is often very institutional. Your projects are atmospheric, using organic materials and textures. Is this instinctive for you?

CAM It is instinctive to a point. The tectonics and the construction itself can create a positive experience of the building. Today we live in a world with a proliferation of generic spaces that do not have much character in material terms. There are two interesting aspects here. One is variation in scale: avoiding tall, monumental, cold spaces, so there can be an alternate perception of higher spaces in the main rooms of a building and then smaller spaces in the transition areas. The other is a nonsequential set of rooms that you may visit in different pathways and configurations. You can stop and come back. It is not a predetermined route.

Clearly, nature is your friend in Brazil. It's your superpower. Your museums and galleries, especially in Inhotim, are embedded in nature. What opportunities does environmental consciousness bring to museum design?

PZC At our Museu do Pontal, in Rio de Janeiro, which is devoted to folk art, some of the collection did not require the usual strict controls on temperature and humidity. Even in a hot city like Rio we could develop natural ventilation solutions that guarantee comfort for visitors most of the year. And that also guarantees for the museum an energy bill that is compatible with its budget, along with addressing environmental concerns. This is a very practical aspect I would mention.

Can we recycle and adapt more buildings to be museums? When is it even justified to build a new building?
CAM You come from a place where this is already a reality. We in Brazil in twenty years will see a decrease in the population. We are already 80 percent urban. We have lots of good modern buildings built seventy or eighty years ago that are starting the process of obsolescence. Instead of building new buildings, we are interested in converting these sometimes abandoned buildings. Pinacoteca is a case in point. The new structure was a listed building, but empty, almost abandoned. And the question was how we could change the original use, which was a school, and transform it into a museum. We created spaces for exhibitions and collections, but we were especially interested in how this intervention could revitalize the building and its context— to think of this process as a means of creating infrastructure for a public, open, democratic museum.

Speaking of visual messages, some museums represent what they are about—an art museum that looks like a giant brushstroke— while others use a more neutral language. Where do you stand?
CAM In between. Not so iconic, but with specificity in materials. We believe people should always remember the place where they have been. The museum should not be a void, a completely inexpressive space. We can balance specificity in terms of experience with a greater range of possibilities in appropriation and use. That is our challenge.

Even as the field shifts away from the grand gestures of post-Bilbao starchitecture, museums still need to signal that these are important civic spaces, not merely ordinary buildings. That is a complicated balancing act, no?
PZC Exactly. We should try to avoid this iconic and monumental architecture. But then we have this new challenge: to seek a more welcoming and recognizable building, as a

Paula Zasnicoff Cardoso & Carlos Alberto Maciel

place where you can be, but without forgetting it—still keeping it in memory.

CAM Welcoming, memorable, open, delicate, but memorable.

You are a collective of architects. What is your process for designing a museum?

PZC Any architectural process is necessarily interdisciplinary and involves many professions and specificities. I would also mention the care we take to listen to all the agents involved in the role of the museum. The management of the building after its construction will be easier if the process includes this listening before we start developing the project. So we usually work with a whole team of people involved in the museum management during the architectural process. And we listen to the community, especially via the educational area of the museum.

I would like to end with Brazil, which seems to be a petri dish of all that is good and troublesome about the world these days. It is a beautiful, multicultural country with authoritarian politics and grave environmental threats. Given all this, what do you consider to be the most urgent priority for museum architecture?

CAM Inclusion and sustainability, a kind of ecological way of building, operating, and being in the world—not only in material terms, but in social terms as well.

PZC And especially in social terms. A museum building has a lot of potential to play a role in inclusion. We have to try to make spaces for that to happen.

DAVID ADJAYE
Adjaye Associates, London, New York City, Accra

THIS PLACE IS ESSENTIAL TO FORMING A HUMAN BEING

It was raining in Washington, D.C., as I approached the National Museum of African American History and Culture. The building's glistening, bronze-coated aluminum wrapping emitted a lantern-like glow against the darkened sky. Its filigreed perforations bristle with allusions to African American craftsmanship, while its sawtooth corners play a melody of call-and-response with the adjacent Washington Monument. Brash yet poetic, the structure cuts a form unlike any of the other institutions silhouetted on the skyline of the National Mall. The fusion of cultural specificity and universal design language is a hallmark of the Ghanaian-British architect David Adjaye. Steeped in London's creative subcultures—his first commissions were artists' homes and studios—Adjaye, now in his mid-fifties, is among the most prolific and outspoken museum makers of his generation. His large project rising in Benin City, Nigeria—a museum to house objects plundered during Africa's colonial past—exemplifies the powerful convictions that animate his work.

History

The future

colonialism.

Dan ... 10/9/2022.

ANDRÁS SZÁNTÓ *I recently visited your museum in Washington, D.C., the National Museum of African American History and Culture. In New York, we're waiting for the completion of your new building for the Studio Museum in Harlem. What was the first museum project you worked on, and which ones are you working on right now?*

DAVID ADJAYE The Museum of Contemporary Art in Denver was the first new-build contemporary art museum I worked on. Right now, we are working on the Princeton University Art Museum; the Edo Museum of West African Art (EMOWAA), in Benin City; and a new museum for an important collector in Delhi, the Kiran Nadar Museum of Art.

Do you remember your first visit to a museum?

I remember visiting the Cairo Museum when my father took me to Egypt. We went to see the Pyramids, and we saw all the sites in Giza. I particularly remember spending time at the museum and being completely blown away by it—a treasure house of things that were left for people to wander through and imagine.

You are an architect with an artist's sensitivity. You came out of the London art scene. You have collaborated with Chris Ofili, Theaster Gates, and Olafur Eliasson. You have designed studios for several artists, one near my house in Brooklyn. Next year in St. Louis, you will present your first public artwork. How has this connection influenced your outlook?

My deep relationship with museums and artists started when I was thinking about my own career. While still a student, I became enmeshed with an incredible group of creative people in London: budding artists, sculptors, painters, conceptualists, jewelry designers. I had found my tribe. I was surrounded by young artists who were desperate to put a fire under the world. They soon started to buy homes and build their own studios. I was part of the gang, and that set up my career. Artists' studios and homes were really my founding soup. If you work with an artist in their studio, you really get to understand how art is made—the struggle, the research, the duration.

I'm always struck by how much of the reality of the studio is missing from the experience of a museum. Much of that open-endedness, that messiness, is sanitized and erased. Why is that?
Because the history of the museum is different from the history of art. The museum is a political project. It has dark roots in the colonial past, an imperial period. The museum had wonderful associations with the Enlightenment, but it was also about empire and power. So for me, the museum is a typologically tainted project, a wounded animal from day one. It celebrates something that it should be mournful about: the targeted destruction of some societies. Yet at its core, the idea of sharing knowledge is fundamentally beautiful. In the end, the museum is a machine that teaches people about the world. But at what price?

You were born to Ghanaian parents in Tanzania, and Africa is a huge part of your life and work. Can you speak a little about the Edo Museum of West African Art, the most ambitious museum project on the continent, and its central role in current debates about restitution?
Benin City for West Africa is like Athens for Europe. It is the cultural hub that influenced all the different royal families and tribes and cultural tropes that we now understand to be West African. The project began more than ten years ago with the Benin Dialogue Group, a collective of museum directors from around the world who were talking through the process of restitution for the artifacts that belonged to that great kingdom.

The thinking behind EMOWAA is that bringing the objects back should allow the communities that once owned them to activate their own modernity and emancipation—their reckoning about where they are in their present. The tropes of your ancestors are critical to your identity and your future. The colonial project destroyed the physical fabric of West Africa. All that is left is these objects. Our thought is that the museum of the Global South would be about restitution, education, relational operations, a kind of a return of the heart of the community.

The museum was born in Europe and raised in America. Recently it has been expanding in Asia and the Middle East. Yet in the next century Africa may be one of its main areas of growth. What will that mean for museums?

It aligns perfectly with the trajectory of the continent. The museum is a means by which to resuscitate the identity of the African continent, as the keeper and re-imaginer of a new relationship with patrimonial artifacts. It can also speak to a new architectural identity, a new imagining of the city, a new civilization in the modern world.

African cities are still playing catch-up and, too often, trying to mimic the West. I believe you need certain typologies to resuscitate the city, and the museum is one of them. It is a condenser of cultural potential. You can make the museum a reference point for how you start to think about growth.

There is a strain of museum-making that has long leaned into these yearnings. Many architects point to museums like MASP in São Paulo, the Centre Pompidou, and the Louisiana as points of departure, as DNA strands to build on.

One hundred percent. And you can add the National Museum of Anthropology in Mexico City. A whole strand of incredible museums can be found in post-colonial cities and in countries that have had a strange relationship to the dominant European powers. I love Finland and Denmark for that. There is a different relationship to the epicenter of the pure colonial project, which has forced those places to create their own unique typological models. You can definitely say that my generation recognizes this clearly. I definitely do.

Imagine new versions now on the African continent, a continent with seven distinct regions, each with its own myriad microcosms of diversity. I see a potential for seven great museums at a minimum to evolve in Africa, but really maybe as many as seven hundred.

Let's talk for a second about starchitecture and where we are right now in the history of the museum. The period after the 1990s was a time of the museum as a work of art.

David Adjaye

I call it the distraction period. Distraction from a sense of hopelessness. You have got to make something extraordinary to stop people from looking at the content.

This approach took over from previous models of impressive museum architecture: Modernist palaces and, going back further in time, neoclassical temples of the muses—all of them exuding a Eurocentric cultural authority. Lately, we seem to be moving toward different modes of cultural relevance.

Totally. The internet era has lifted the shroud of content and meaning, so the public are no longer just a herd of sheep that simply follows the museum as the arbiter of truth. People now search for things that interest them in the museum. And that has had a huge impact on the standing of museums in the world, on their cultural relevance. Museums had long tried not to respond to this situation. But now they simply must respond.

I see two dominant trends: On the one hand, there is the entrenchment of the classical public museum as this holy temple that is revered and almost made into a sacred object. On the other hand, the museum has exploded into the private realm, with many new buildings financed by philanthropists who collect privately, and who are creating their own narratives, apart from national narratives. So you get both ends: the reverence for the holy tropes of a certain world, and the new diversities, the new relational moments and hierarchies.

For me what is more interesting is the disaggregation of these monolithic collecting forms. A more interesting strategy would be a collaborative relational system that starts to see the museum as a globally decentralized nodal network, one that can speak about world culture rather than reinforcing the colonial idea of "you have to come to London and Paris to really understand what culture is." It would be more radical if these institutions, which keep 95 percent of their collections in boxes, created networks of relationships that could speak collectively about the ability for humans to understand their histories and cultures. That would be my preferred model for dissolving this nonsense of one place and one hierarchy.

So with that multinodal network in mind, how would you define a museum?

For me, the museum has to be taken off the pedestal of high culture and put on the pedestal of everyday culture. It is the cultural community center of any agglomeration of human beings—their forum, their reception room, and their public room.

Let's talk about this new "public room." To move in this direction, what does the museum need to unlearn?

We have made the museum feel as though it is the teacher of culture for us. At the heart of that process is a flawed relationship. We have somehow given up our ability to understand that culture is made in the community. The relationship between the community and its archive needs to be realigned. The museum is a depository, but also a place of active imagination. It is a place that allows us to remember lost histories and to bring them back to us, to go as far back as we can go. And one that allows us to imagine a possible future.

I remember a Studio Museum exhibition you organized in 2007 about public spaces. What can museums learn from other public venues you have designed, like churches and libraries?

Those typologies are also undergoing massive reinvention. The three together are the archetypal triptych of the city—the church, the library, and the museum—and all three are rethinking their conditions.

The library, in its purest form, was about access to hidden knowledge. The elite library—the monastery library, the private castle library—has evolved into the public library and democratized itself. The church used to be about priests presiding over the congregation, and this too has shifted to a more collective ambience, where the call-and-response of the citizenry actively manifests a chamber in which a certain equality of performer and receiver prevails. In other words, auditoriums and theaters in the round have taken over.

All institutions are contending with the repercussions of the internet age, which has completely challenged the singularity of authority, and correspondingly forced architecture to rethink

David Adjaye

how the stage is set for a believable engagement between experts and citizens.

Many museums aspire now to shift toward this less hierarchical model. But an architect must turn it into reality. How can I tell when a museum is meeting this standard?
You can't do it with the old architecture. In libraries, you find moms and teenagers and pensioners in one corner and academics at the top. When you have that mix, you know you have created an irreplicable relationship with your community. It has to be a multigenerational relationship. The museum has to crack that code. From the elderly to the toddlers, there must be a symbiotic sense that this place is essential to forming a human being. The architecture has to show that. An architecture structured to see the world a certain way, that refuses to allow multiple viewpoints or to engage with dissolving the hierarchy, smells like a rat to citizens. There will be a mistrust, no matter how much you repaper the veneer of the program. We believe in things because of space. Architecture makes people believe things—that is one of its most profound powers.

Let me dig into your image of a multigenerational utopia. What are the specific tools, materials, spatial configurations, that can get you there? I'm waiting for that little book of rules.
A rule book would set up a dangerous precedent of laziness. The answer is the endpoint. Any architect worth the name should understand how to analyze those moments and construct a relational, spatial condition to create that transmission. For me, the skill is having the ability to understand how to allow people to evolve and be more responsive.

Much of this is about how space is apportioned in the museum. How do you view the relationship between public space and exhibition space?
It is about desacralizing and making the relationship horizontal. The idea that there is a sacred temple, and then there is this profane space of debate and discussion, is fundamentally problematic. Only very few objects in a museum require a sacred moment—the lost object, the last one. Everywhere else you try

to create relational proximity to all the objects. The objects have to somehow operate as information.

The unique power of the museum is that it offers another way into human intelligence, one that is beyond language—a landscape of surface texture, duration, and spatial sequence that generates a neural uplift and understanding that we can thrive on.

The new public room must engage the society around it, yet to some extent it should also offer shelter from it. Some people want the museum to be a platform for political debates. Others feel it should be a sanctuary, a refuge. Where do you land?
Both positions are romantic. Neither one is what the public room is about. If you understand the public room as the archive, as the relational engagement with different forms of communication, understanding, ability, then you realize that you are entering an arena that is oscillating between information that is happening in the world, while being processed into a certain condition, distillation, and concretization to communicate certain essential ideas. It cannot be just a sanctuary, or a place where you go to make a political rally. That is simply not what it is set up to do. In the future, if we build hundreds of these archives, some might be spaces where we can make a political statement, and some may not.

I want to ask about the future—and don't say you don't deal with the future, because every architect is a futurologist.
We all are. If you don't believe that, then you're not an architect. You must be a futurologist.

So then how, ultimately, will tomorrow's museums look and feel? If I walk into a museum of tomorrow—maybe one of those seven major ones in Africa—what will surprise me about it?
The ability for these places to be at once incredible containers of multigenerational artifacts, information, and production, as well as places for the engagement of citizens in their own self-discovery and identity as people of their world and the time they are living in.

What is your approach to designing a museum? Once invited, how do you proceed, and whom do you listen to?
Each project is an experiment. Each one is an incredible respon-

David Adjaye

sibility to allow the evolution of the art form. Small or large, each project is an iterative process that offers the great privilege of building on a body of knowledge—in a sort of avalanche. I listen to a lot of artists, a lot of dear friends who are close to me. Artists are my primary sounding boards for my ideas. And increasingly, as I get older, I listen to myself.

In an interview for Artforum, *you once said, "Many contemporary museums fall flat because they end up with something generic—they become dead spaces."*[1] *How can museum architecture avoid that generic condition?*
When I said that, some people felt I was trying to make an argument for spectacle. I have no interest in spectacle for spectacle's sake. What I am always searching for in a museum is how to extend its mission toward a greater understanding of what a particular place is about, and how to form a unique space that talks about its history and how it engages with the modernity that is all around us. I am arguing for more specificity.

We are meeting in difficult times. The globalist project is in question. Institutional authority is in question. Social peace is in question. Yet we have this institution, the museum, that somehow can be a uniter, a convener, a mediator. How do you situate the architect in that picture?
The architect is a critical player—unfortunately, sometimes a player that has been a guilty culprit in the projection of the propaganda of the museum. We need some humility in understanding exactly what a museum represents in our society, and how we can make it as relevant as possible for the generations to come.

I will give you an example that may surprise you. I frequently refer back to Sir John Soane's Museum, in London—the idea of the museum as the house of a person, with a display of a particular mind that has been made in a particular context. That specificity has more charm and attraction; it generates greater engagement and a deeper desire to learn than we find in most museums. The idea of being invited into that kind of house is more interesting to me than visiting a generic institution.

1. Julian Rose, "Living Spaces: An Interview with David Adjaye," *Artforum*, October 2017.

KERSTIN THOMPSON
Kerstin Thompson Architects, Melbourne

WHERE DOES THE MUSEUM BEGIN AND END?

One day I hope to visit Bundanon, an arts complex situated on a large tract of preternaturally beautiful land about two hours south of Sydney, Australia. It is here that Kerstin Thompson and her team of Melbourne-based architects have conceived a series of culturally and environmentally sensitive inter-ventions, in the form of an underground museum and a muscular bridge formed with a latticework of black steel beams that functions as an artist-residency facility. But to appreciate these structures solely for their visual acumen would be to miss the point. The choices behind them reveal respect for First Nations knowledge linked to the site, as well as for the exigencies of its ecology, already bruised by climate change. In this and other cultural projects, Thompson, whose practice extends to landscape and interior design, demonstrates a flair for testing the conventions of museum architecture. For her, the museum should soften up both its external and self-imposed internal boundaries.

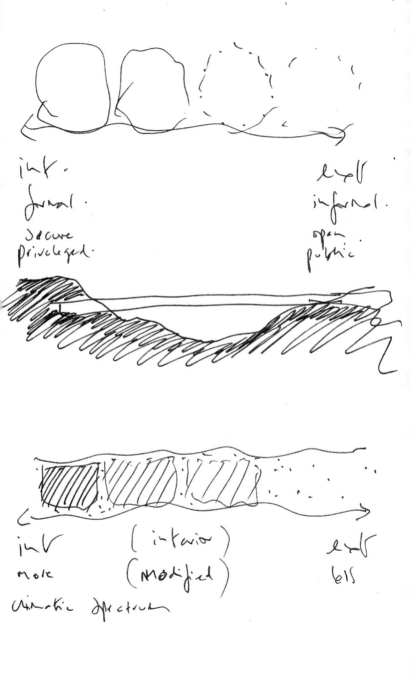

int.

formal.
secure
privileged.

end
informal.
open.
public

int
more
climatic spectrum

(interior)
(modified)

end
less

ANDRAS SZÁNTÓ *Tell me about the Bundanon Art Museum and The Bridge, a remarkable structure that you designed in Southeast Australia.*

KERSTIN THOMPSON Bundanon is a large estate on bush that was gifted to the Australian people in 1993 by one of our renowned painters, Arthur Boyd. He lived and painted there with his family for twenty years and amassed a collection of works by himself and his peers. It has been running education and residency programs for a long time, and they needed more facilities. The intent was to build a museum and additional accommodation—The Bridge—so they could expand the number of students and residents.

Bundanon's landscape is deeply impacted by climate change. The site has had two huge flood events already this year. Two years ago bushfires came close and they had to evacuate the collection. The new museum and collection storage are built as a subterranean space and therefore resistant to fire. The bridge is about flood resilience. So while it offers a remarkable experience in a beautiful part of the world, Bundanon is also a model for how you might build in landscapes that are under all sorts of serious threats from climate change.

That's quite a statement about the museum of the future—its need for protection against floods and fires. Are you working on museum projects right now?

The first time we contemplated the museum was for Monash University Museum of Art (MUMA), around 2011. We are now working on TarraWarra Museum of Art, a private museum in a wine estate outside Melbourne. We are adding a companion building to the museum, an education space, and open collection storage, all underground. We seem to be specializing in underground museums. They are interesting, too, because by being underground they have a passive thermal stability. They reduce the mechanical servicing required as well as being fire-resistant.

It's impossible to think about Australia without its landscape and its connection to First Nations' practices. How does that color your outlook on museums and their architecture?

At Bundanon, we were interested in landscape not just in the

Kerstin Thompson

picturesque sense. We tried to think of it as part of an extended landscape system, the Shoalhaven region, which is a big water-catchment area. The landscape is structured around wet and dry gullies and river systems and tributaries, so water flow was a huge part of the site and how it performs. The bridge component is all about celebrating that aspect and working with the flows of the site, rather than understanding architecture only as this beautiful thing in a beautiful setting.

Bundanon Trust has a close relationship with the First Nations peoples of Dharawal Country, the Wodi Wodi and the Yuin peoples. Understanding and appreciating the impact of fire and inundation is one of the ways in which the buildings attempt to respect and engage with First Nations' knowledge of the site. Because, of course, *flood* is an anthropocentric term—it's only when settlements are inundated that this overflow is labeled a flood. Here we speak about "inundation," which is a natural and important part of this landscape. That is why the project has purposefully allowed these flows to continue.

That's a level of thinking we don't yet have in the US. Your practice, which you established in 1994, does architecture, landscape, urban design, and interiors. You also teach. What's the common thread linking these endeavors?
They are all continuous. The boundaries between them frustrate me. When I was studying in the late 1980s and early 1990s, we read a lot about post-structuralism, a lot about undoing of boundaries, if you like. That interest in gray zones and in-between conditions continues for me. When it comes to museums, one thing that continues to surprise me is why we still have such a binary thinking about museum spaces. They are very particularly controlled climatically inside, with social functions relegated to outside. I know that is partly about loan agreements being tied to thermal conditions. But we could imagine more of a continuum between inside and outside. It is strange that we have yet to see many buildings that respond to this much greater range of conditions for art practice.

Which museum buildings do you admire the most? Which ones shaped your sense of a great museum?

I have a strong attachment to the Centre Pompidou, probably from personal experience. In 1987, I was living in Europe and I spent time in Paris. I remember the library more than the museum. I would go there to read and walk around, because you could just hang out there. When I was back in Paris, in 2003, the Palais de Tokyo had just been opened up after Lacaton & Vassal's renovation. Again, what I enjoyed was the looseness. They had a tight budget, so they did more editing than adding. I remember the café as part of the lobby space. It was teeming with young people who looked like they used the museum to hang out on a regular basis. That intrigued me. I liked its unpreciousness, its rawness. It challenged notions about the white-walled museum. I must say, it's hard to get curators to move away from that model.

I often say the white cube is a period room. It belongs to a certain moment. So where exactly are we today in museum architecture? We've left behind the museum as temple. The Pompidou was not a temple; it was a town square. Then came the statement museums of the 1990s and the Bilbao Effect—the museum as work of art. How would you describe this moment?
There is a tension between the purpose-built, "high" architecture museums, on the one hand, and on the other hand spaces that have adapted their original purpose and have become temporary galleries or museums. Reusing such spaces gets us used to seeing art outside environments specifically designed for it. One example is a nineteenth-century Victorian hotel in Melbourne called The Windsor. It has seen better days. Lately, it has occasionally functioned as a companion venue to the Melbourne Art Fair. Having galleries set up hotel rooms with art is fantastic—a fascinating way to take artworks out of their conventional context.

That's the art world. We'll take anything. Give us a hospital. A jail. A factory. We will turn it into a museum. I don't know another civic institution that does that. So with all that in mind, how would you define museums?
I think of them as becoming slightly messier. While museums have always done a lot of things, nowadays we expect them

Kerstin Thompson

to do even more. They seem profoundly social. People are more comfortable being up-front about the social aspect of the museum as a primary reason for going—a museum as a means of engaging with one another. By messier I also mean the shifts in relation to front-of-house and back-of-house, which used to be quarantined. While that separation is still the norm, you see more moves to reveal what's hidden in storage, for instance.

The museum is one of the last institutions to maintain this front stage/backstage separation. In restaurants forty years ago the kitchens were hidden. Once they opened them up, the chefs became stars, and people are now obsessed with cuisine. And the kitchens are cleaner.

Fair point. But doubling back to sociability, another institution I love is the Louisiana in Denmark. We went there on a Thursday night, when they had their weekly Smorgasbord event. People come, whole families, multigenerational, for a reasonably priced dinner, and then they can just wander around the museum, till quite late. That struck me as a fantastic model for opening up the museum to a wider demographic—exceeding the usual time boundaries, too. That informality is quite important.

As an architect and a citizen, what are some things that frustrate you about museums?

Let's go back to climate control. A museum project that always intrigued me was submitted by Fake Industries for the never-completed Guggenheim Helsinki competition. Rather than being fixated on exterior form, walls, and formal spaces of the museum, they emphasized the importance of interiority in Helsinki and proposed a spectrum of internal climate conditions. What opportunities would open up if we were less compartmentalized in our relationship to climate? Of course, most gallery people would be mortified by that suggestion. It relates to this disconnect between where art and sociability in the museum take place. Being shoehorned into spaces that are still largely legacies of nineteenth-century Beaux Arts—the studio with clerestory windows—is a frustration.

This brings us to placemaking. The museum should have a strong sense of place. How can architecture support that?

I thought about this explicitly when designing MUMA, which was relocating from a suburban to an urban location. We proposed that you could use the museum to repair the campus. Let's try to drag the museum program out into the external spaces of the campus and activate them—to embed the museum into people's everyday habits. Even if students had no intention of going inside, something about the museum would still be part of their experience. We pushed for the museum to be brought out into a forecourt for external performances and works—also a lovely landscape for people to hang out in. We added large windows that allow you to look into the guts of the museum. We turned the museum inside out, so that it could be available without having to enter, incidental to everyday campus life. That was the beginning of my interest in the museum as a means for placemaking.

I would like to unpack what makes for a sense of place, and specifically a space for community. This is a central discussion in museums today. Are there good examples?

The Pompidou is an obvious one: the plaza as an extension of activities associated with it. It is important that it can be taken over by a non-museum program. We did a competition for a gallery in Shepparton, which is situated in parkland. We suggested that you would literally walk through the museum every day. If you were walking your dog, you would walk through the museum. The Garage Museum campus, in Moscow, is an example of this accessibility, although you still have a strong threshold dividing inside and outside. At OMA's Kunsthal Rotterdam, the architecture creates a ramped pathway from street to park. As you move through, you get to see inside a lecture theater. You pass through the museum en route to something else. But even then you still have a glass wall, a defined boundary, as well as hours of operation that delimit access. This is an architectural problem to some extent, but also an operational or management problem.

Sense of place is partly about atmosphere. Museums tend to exude a mood of lofty authority. They can be rather cold and institutional. How can you get the tonality right?

Kerstin Thompson

Funnily enough, the acoustic qualities are really important. Even in the whitest, hardest of cube spaces, you can undermine the pristineness with a more comforting, gentle experience. That is something architects don't talk about enough. Acoustic experience is subliminal. Improving the sound feel can be a good way of bringing people in without their even realizing it. Likewise, in Bundanon, from time to time they have a day when the lights are set lower. It's about creating a softer experience.

Let's linger on light, another subliminal driver of the experience.
That's another frustration, this generic approach to light— another white cube diminishing the context and any signs of where you might actually be in the world. At Bundanon, a lot of the works in the collection were painted in daylight and are best seen in daylight. So we introduced skylights to show them in a naturally lit space, while also allowing the museum to shut that down (via bushfire shutters) and fully use artificial lighting. I would love to imagine that one day the light in the gallery is just the light we get on any given day. And if it's a dark day, so be it.

As with the climate zones in Helsinki, you could go with different light zones.
Yes, dark and moody. Wouldn't that be interesting?

You are a prolific designer of sublime domestic and commercial interiors. We know the interiors that make people feel comfortable and content. It's no mystery. We know them from hotels and residential architecture and even boutiques. Why aren't these moods more frequently used in museums?
It's interesting, isn't it? I can speculate about it. In many traveling exhibitions you see the white cube being repainted dark blue, or whatever, because they are trying to reinstate a character that is a counterpoint or a complement to the work. It's like this whole question of character has been asked to be excised from the museum project. Maybe it is time to challenge it more. I am surprised that more gallery or museum directors haven't thought about challenging it. They are still trapped in these protocols, these accepted conventions that are slow to shift.

Perhaps it's about positioning the museum outside of everyday life—a twentieth-century way of signaling a sacred space. If you make the museum feel too everyday, you dilute the mission. Let's go back to the question of balancing public spaces versus gallery spaces.

I am fascinated by gray zones—I'm going to have to say "spectrum," really. Spectrums are more interesting than the poles at either end. There is no reason you couldn't have a lot of artworks in more explicitly public space. You could just curate and create according to the spaces on offer and respond to their different opportunities. I imagine there are certain artworks that could be in outdoor spaces and subject to weather and deterioration, and that is just part of the deal. I am surprised that even works around climate are still usually made with "permanent"-based practices, like video, that don't allow them to be more fully site-specific by being reactive to, changed by, the dynamics of the situation, the climate. There are enormous opportunities there.

You are deeply involved in landscape design. It seems that landscape has largely been an afterthought for cultural institutions. How should it be applied to museums?

It's about continuum. Where does the museum begin and end? Some would say it starts on your phone when you book a ticket. Landscape is part of that lead-up, whether it is a rural landscape or an urban one. All of that is part of the experience. It needs to be considered or anticipated. At Bundanon, from the moment you turn off the highway and drive through the bush and approach the site, you slowly get little reveals of the building, and you get to the car park, and then walk from the car park to the museum proper, crossing a pedestrian bridge over the creek—all of these are opportunities to talk about the situation that is fundamental to how the visitor is going to experience the museum itself and the works in it. It is not a passive landscape. It is an active participant.

So how, ultimately, will tomorrow's museums surprise us? How do you imagine them to be different?

It will be interesting to see how the digital and the virtual dimension of the museum play out. What has been interesting—maybe accounting for the increasingly social aspects of museums—is

Kerstin Thompson

this profound need for people now to be in shared space. It will continue to be important to be physically grounded, somehow. But that is not to say that museums couldn't be more sneaky. When we say, "We are going to a museum today," at that moment we know we are going into a place with boundaries. Yet I can imagine how, with better technology, there could be more art experiences that are incidental to daily life, somehow woven into it. Art practices that we might normally reserve for museum spaces may someday become more part of everyday life.

It seems like architects and designers will have to invent a new language for a virtual museum space.
Because of Covid-19, we have seen the limits of the virtual. Digital space makes the incidental so much more difficult. That's where physical space becomes so important. For example, we have been working on a future court building, and one thing that has been tested during Covid is the absence of physical spaces like the corridor, shared zones where unplanned meetings between lawyers in passing enable the opportunistic making of a deal. In the online environment, they had to formalize that interaction. There is something to be said for connections that only happen because you share a space. This informality is hard to achieve online, and so is the vulnerability that goes along with it. That is why physical space has a good future.

What a relief. Let's end with some advice for the next generation. What do you say to a young architect starting out today who is aspiring to design museums for the future?
A few things. The figure of the architect and of the older museum does need to be challenged. Architects need to be more open and listen to what the people who will eventually use these spaces have to say about them. The term *accommodation* can be seen as passive, but I think the act of accommodating can be a generative and proactive gesture as well, especially when there is a clear intent behind it. Some older ways of working in architecture had a dogmatic aspect, in order to get these revered buildings built. I think now and in the future we will be able to make very clear buildings with great integrity through a much more open and accommodating process.

DAVID CHIPPERFIELD
David Chipperfield Architects, London, Berlin,
Milan, Shanghai

EVERYTHING IS SENSITIZED

My first visit to Berlin's Neues Museum, around 2010,
was an emotionally charged experience. Revived by
British architect David Chipperfield more than a
half-century after being reduced to a ruin, the structure
doesn't shy away from its traumatic past. "How do
you deal with history?" the building seems to ask.
Chipperfield's poetic answer was to leave untouched
the remnants of the original structure that had survived the war. With its walls of bare brick, charred
stuccos, and countless other exposed wounds, the new
Neues put forward a fresh vocabulary. It is a memo-
rial as much as a museum. For Chipperfield, whose
five-decade career has encompassed many influential
museum assignments—from the light-touch renovation of Ludwig Mies van der Rohe's Neue Nationalgalerie, also in Berlin, to the robust travertine tower
of Museo Jumex in Mexico City—each project is a
question waiting to be answered. Common to all is
his desire to create experiences of belonging, contemplation, and comfort.

ANDRÁS SZÁNTÓ *Your architecture often reflects on history, so let's start there. Six weeks ago, on March 2, your firm suspended work in Russia. You announced online, "As a practice we believe in dialogue, openness, and engagement, values that are directly opposed to the ongoing war." Architects sometimes work in close proximity to power. What is the responsibility of the architect in a moment like this?*

DAVID CHIPPERFIELD We don't *sometimes* work in close proximity to power. We *always* work in proximity to power of some sort. We are not writers or painters. We can't just go home and make a house or a museum on our own. Instead, we are dependent on a large team and access to resources, including money and power, to create our work. This can be hard to navigate sometimes.

My career coincides with the demise of the welfare state and the more engaged attitude of professionals that emerged in the UK after World War II. The generation of architects that taught me worked on social housing, university campuses, schools, etc., often working directly within government or local authorities. Under Margaret Thatcher's government the process of dismantling this welfare state began, and with it came privatization, a shift for the profession of architecture. Now we invest so much time in self-promotion, appealing to investors and courting wealth, in order to get work. The generation before us would never have accepted this level of self-promotion, but we have to consider our relationship to power and our societal role.

On the bright side, you started your practice in 1985, just ahead of a great global opening. You have offices in London, Berlin, Milan, Shanghai. Overall, has this been a good time to be an architect?

For those of us who were fortunate, it was a good time. As we look back on the past forty years, there were some very good buildings, and increasingly so. In the late 1970s and 1980s, the steam had run out of the modern movement. You cannot deny that there has been a great generation of architects in the past forty years who have put a focus on buildings of high quality, whether you like them or not.

David Chipperfield

You have worked on iconic museums, like the Neue National-galerie and the Neues Museum. You have added to existing museums from St. Louis to Zürich. And you have created new ones, like the Museo Jumex in Mexico City. Through all this, what has informed your own understanding of museums?
Every museum is different. When we worked on the Museum Folkwang, in Essen, I looked at a number of other new museums as part of the design process. I realized that their architecture irritated me. It's not that I don't want to see other architects do different things, but I was irritated in terms of the museum experience, and by the fact that so many museum buildings were following a brief to become spectacles in them-selves and attract a large number of people.

It all started with the Guggenheim Bilbao. All of a sudden the museum was embedded in the tourism business. And you end up with another power alliance, where culture is trying to make itself valid based on the measurements of consumer society. Visitor numbers become the measure of everything. Then the museum becomes part of an urban-regeneration program, validated by cities' desire to renew themselves. But ultimately you have to first want a museum for its core task—which is to be a piece of social and cultural communal infrastructure, first and foremost for the people who live around it, not tourists.

After Bilbao we saw the rise of the museum as a kind of spectacle. How do you arrive at the right kind of museum?
I think I can be clear: I do not believe that culture is an exotic thing. It should be part of our common infrastructure. We need to celebrate activities that lie beyond the practical and commer-cial ties that bind us together.

From an architect's point of view, the German system is potentially a more comfortable one. It is so professional and regulated. The architect is selected, the feasibility of the project established, the funds placed in a box. There will have been an enormous amount of preparation. You have the security of the machinery of the public administration behind the process. In the US and the UK, there is no such public mechanism. Projects depend on someone donating the money, and you don't always know how much money is out there. You end up trying to work out the parameters of the project while you are working out if there is money out there to build it.

However, this is not always a negative thing. When we worked on the Saint Louis Art Museum, we would present the project to the community every two months, because we needed to gain their support for our proposal. It was not pre-approved, and the museum was engaged in a real dialogue with the city. By the time we finished, the project had been continuously scrutinized, so everybody knew what it was. The strange thing in Germany is that when you finish your museum and open it to the public, relatively few people know what the final building is going to look like, as the emphasis has been on the process rather than the product. Clearly, the ideal process lies somewhere between these two poles.

Still, you have to balance that element of spectacle with the needs of everyday people, who often visit museums as a refuge, a place to get away from it all. How do you create such a sanctuary, a contemplative communal space, with your tools?
Our contemporary life is about distraction and fast pace, and the museum is one of the few places where we are expected to slow down and focus. There are few times when we are happy just alone with our own thoughts—perhaps reading a book, looking at art, or being in a church. I firmly believe this quality should not be lost in museums. You should step into a space, a series of rooms, where your whole performance in relationship to what is around you is different from how you relate to the other spaces of your daily life. Everything is sensitized, visually and aurally. That is an extraordinary task for an architect to play with—to heighten our senses.

The philosopher and critic Arthur C. Danto talked about the "transfiguration of the commonplace" in art. Museum architecture is likewise a transfiguration, in a sense, as it allows you to enter this "sensitized" state. How do you shift people into that mindset?
That transfiguration is done first and foremost by the institution. With the architecture you create for that institution, you

David Chipperfield

can then give more legitimacy to the notion that the things it displays are important.

My first three buildings were in Japan, and I ended up spending six or seven years there. I found that Japanese culture has the ability to make things feel more important. Seemingly innocent things are given value. It is an elevation by context of things we take for granted. And that is what architecture can help you do. Architecture can create a condition of comfort, where you feel like you want to be there. In order to get into the right atmosphere or mood, it is important that you feel happy. In our world of constant movement and appointments, of always looking ahead to doing the next thing, architects can contribute to the feeling that "where I am is where I want to be at this particular moment."

That slowing and focusing of the senses is a kind of poetry. Your renovation of the Neues Museum, I admit, made me cry. My family lived through that history. Leaving it on view, absorbing it rather than hiding it, was a radically poetic gesture. And it could have turned out awfully. Could you reflect on this strategy?
We were restoring the museum fifty years after it had been made a ruin. It had been a ruin for such a significant portion of its lifetime that its identity was a composite of original qualities and what had happened to it over its decades of decay. Yes, it was a ruin, but it had gone back into a sort of geological state, and when you went around it the hairs stood up on your neck. It felt like being in Pompeii.

I wanted to stay close to this combination of history and geology that had chemically emerged from these conditions. I had no idea what the Neues Museum would end up looking like when we started. I just said, "We mustn't remove anything that is standing, nor replace any material that can be saved." This forced us into a very particular way of completion, because normally the opposite approach is applied: to subsume a ruin into a new totality. If you wanted something that looks complete, then you wouldn't do what we did. Members of the Ministry of Finance visited the site toward the end of the project and demanded, "How are we going to explain to people that we put all this money toward this project and you haven't finished it?"

It may be something you can only do once. The second time someone attempts it, it could turn out as kitsch.

There are important lessons we learned through the experience. We depended on process, and for that you have to have real engagement from everyone. I am proud that I was able to build trust among the people who started the project, each one with different ambitions. I was an Englishman coming to a city I didn't know, to a building surrounded by trauma and emotions that I hadn't experienced. I had to listen to everybody continuously. That to me is an aspect of architecture that is profoundly important, and is missing in most of our duties. With the Neues Museum, we were constantly in an open-minded mode. This profoundly informed our process. The work could not have been done by a single architect; it came out of collaboration.

Let's come back to spectacle. You clearly do need some sense of occasion. You don't want the museum to look ordinary. How can architecture provide that specialness without showing off?
When we began this conversation, I was talking about what buildings can do to you experientially when you're walking through their spaces, but you can't only represent this positive aspect inside. So absolutely you need to start thinking about how the architecture should present itself externally. That's probably an architect's most naked moment—when we have to drill down on more personal and somewhat contrived narratives. Sometimes those are contextual; for example, we build the building out of brick because it's a brick city. This is what architects do: We try to justify our aesthetic choices, because we are acutely aware that we will need to explain them. A painter doesn't have to do that.

At the same time, some of the shiny starchitecture of recent decades does make people feel excluded. The fancy design that beckons cultural tourists can make some people feel uninvited. Where does museum architecture go from here?
I am hoping the Covid-19 pandemic changes things. It may give us the opportunity to do things that we were too frightened to do before, because we tended to say, "Well, that's how things

David Chipperfield

are." Now, between Covid-19 and the war in Ukraine, we are increasingly unclear about "how things are." We can ask more fundamental questions. The environmental crisis, too, forces us to ask questions more rigorously than ever before. I would agree with you that brash expressions of showing off are going to look rather silly in the next ten to fifteen years. Architecture as a profession is going to start to redirect itself—it must.

So with all this in mind, how do you define a museum?
I could give you all the conventional answers about building and protecting collections. But reflecting especially on my North American experiences, working on museums from Anchorage to St. Louis, I realize that a museum can be a focus, a sort of social-cultural focus point. In a place like Des Moines, Iowa, a museum can have quite a strong civic role. It can be important for the community's sense of itself.

I have always wanted to write an essay titled "The Mosque, the Mall, and the Museum"—three spaces of congregation for all kinds of people. But in a museum, unlike in a mosque or a mall, there is no obligation to believe or to consume. There are no strings attached.
I have spent the past two years in an isolated rural community in northwestern Spain. I also run a foundation that has been working with the community here for six years. It's quite rural, and a place where the art market hardly exists, although there are plenty of artists here. The relationship between daily life and cultural activity seems slightly more old-fashioned, but it still exists in all sorts of forms. Then you see a place like The Metropolitan Museum of Art, desperately trying to become relevant to diverse histories and thinking more about nontangible heritage, patrimony, diversity, and the importance of community. It's quite interesting to be in a place where none of those anxieties really exist, because they haven't ever been lost.

So how, ultimately, might tomorrow's museums look and feel different? Or in your mind will they fundamentally be made of the same DNA as museums of today?

I think you have to distinguish between museums of artifacts and museums of stories. Science museums and history museums are complicated, because you don't necessarily have objects. Science museums have moved away from being seen as boring cabinets of rocks and fossils, and are now more focused on storytelling. While this perhaps makes them more interactive and exciting, one loses the simplicity of a direct encounter with an object or artifact in the museum. A room full of paintings from the Dutch Golden Age or French Impressionists is unlikely to change much. You will always need walls to hang them on, and spaces of contemplation in which you can admire them.

The change comes from contemporary art shifting its focus from the obsession with surface and material into wider responsibilities of narratives and commentary. As soon as a melting iceberg is a piece of art, then you've got to think about different types of space for a museum experience.

At Museo Jumex, in Mexico City, we consciously added a nonspecific space on the first floor. It is a kind of vitrine, a glass box. While it may not be the ideal space for displaying paintings, it can be used to display installations and host talks and performances, readings, conferences—it really opens up the programming. Contemporary museums and artists will be able to work together more closely on such opportunities. But one has to wonder if artists might break away from the structures of the museum altogether. If fifty people on bicycles going around a city is an artwork, why does it still need to be attached to an institution?

To adapt to a future where art is changing this way and society is changing fast, what does museum architecture need to unlearn the most?
To some degree, museums are going through a sort of reckoning, like all institutions right now. Every company now describes itself as a social service. Even banks are reframing themselves as institutions that "lend money to give people opportunities." Everyone is trying to be virtuous. Everybody is addressing issues of environment, gender, race, inequality—and quite correctly so. The issue is, once museums break out of their

David Chipperfield

box, they might lament how useful the box had been. Because once you put something in the box, it takes on meaning. Once you pull down the temple, you are also undercutting your position to some degree.

Fundamentally, I don't think that museums with big collections will change too much. But I suspect that much more dynamic things will happen within *kunsthalle* institutions that are dedicated to curating particular moments or events. Today, we have more of an event-centered culture. So you will basically have two ways to experience art: by going to a temple-like structure to look at precious things, or by being immersed in an installation, performance, event, or experience.

I would like to close by returning to the role of the architect. In 2019 you wrote, "We often claim that responsibility is in the hands of those who control the transactional commercial and political framework within which we must operate, but for too long we have accepted the paradox of our resistance and complicity, developing narratives that explain away our discomfort."[1] *Where are the hard lines in this respect as we move forward?*
I believe profoundly that the profession of architecture has to realign itself in relation to society. We know that the planet needs us not only to create special things, but to make normal things better, to develop our quality of life that is not dependent on consumerism. We know that inequality is not going to be solved by one sector of society getting richer, with better hotels and taller towers to live in. We are going to have to find ways to deal with parts of society that don't get a fair share. And to be honest, working within the limits of a building is just scratching the surface of what is necessary. We are all embedded in a system that is failing, and it can be quite difficult to saw the legs off the chair you're sitting on.

1. David Chipperfield, "What is Our Role?" *Domus*, December 2019.

JING LIU & FLORIAN IDENBURG
SO – IL, New York City

ARCHITECTURE SHOULD ACCOMMODATE A CENTURY OF IDEAS

On a gritty stretch of Downtown Brooklyn, wedged between a Big & Tall boutique and a hair-braiding salon, hides the entrance of the SO – IL architecture studio. A narrow flight of stairs leads to a space crammed with desks and maquettes. A neon sign displays a single word: *future*. I arrived in early 2022 for one of the first conversations in this book, but the studio was almost empty—the pandemic was lurking. Partners in life and work, Jing Liu and Florian Idenburg met while working for SANAA. Since launching SO – IL in 2008, they have carved out a presence in Brooklyn—where their multifunctional Amant Foundation art campus opened in 2021—and beyond. From Hong Kong's K11 Art and Cultural Centre to the Art Mill in Doha, their buildings probe what a contemporary art space can be. Our conversation delved into how museums should be conceived with time in mind, open to a future that cannot be defined.

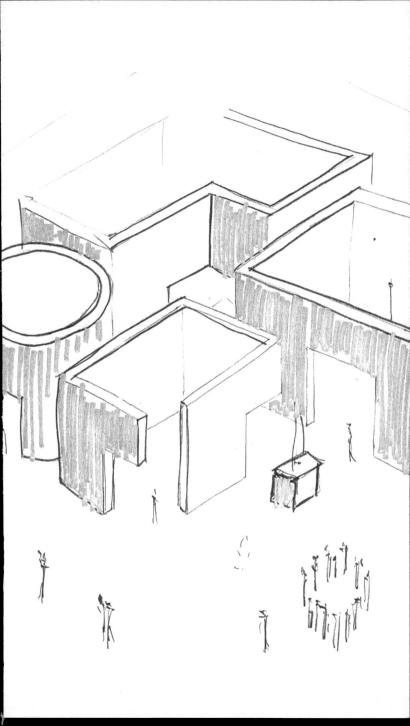

ANDRÁS SZÁNTÓ *As designers, you are deeply concerned with politics, global narratives, and societal engagement. Your team speaks a dozen languages. We're meeting on the ninth day of the war in Ukraine. How does this inform your sense of the responsibility of architecture?*

JING LIU Florian and I grew up in the '80s and '90s, and we have changed our cultural context, where we live, and the language we speak so many times. One thing that has informed our thinking is that change is a constant. That is the richness and strength of this world. Change is something we have to embrace, as architects. However, as architects and as culture-makers, we find that it's not easy to say that culture and history are always changing. What then is the architectural answer?

What was the first museum project you worked on together?
FLORIAN IDENBURG We met working on a museum project with the Japanese architecture firm SANAA, for the Glass Pavilion at the Toledo Museum of Art, in Ohio.

I've been there. A wonderful building.
FI That was the first project I led at SANAA for a museum. But I often say that I was born in a museum. My mother was a docent who spent much of her time in Teylers Museum, the oldest museum in the Netherlands. Recently, we have been involved in projects that are museum-like, but also start to question the definition of a museum. We are moving away from the traditional idea of the museum, to spaces for ideas. We are often involved in designing these nontraditional arts spaces.

Were there any buildings that shaped your understanding of a great museum?
FI When I was working at SANAA, they built the 21st Century Museum of Contemporary Art in Kanazawa, Japan. That museum is based on the idea of relational aesthetics: that an institution could find at its core the establishment of relationships. This idea of establishing relationships—between people and ideas, people and people, people and space—is still part of how we work.

Jing Liu & Florian Idenburg

JL On the other end of the spectrum, the Guggenheim Bilbao was being built around the same time. So on the one hand, you had a discourse about a place where events and relationships happen. On the other hand, you had the strategy of inserting something into the landscape that pivots the conversation completely, because of the sheer presence of the thing. Both approaches informed our thinking about cultural institutions and their role in the city.

Inserting something big: that may be the essence of starchitecture. Perhaps we are moving away from that sense of awe?
FI The pendulum is swinging. We started our practice in 2008, when Barack Obama was elected president. The then-popular idea of an interconnected world produced us as well, as two people from different sides of the globe forming an office in New York, in a way. In recent years, conversations have tilted to local, smaller communities. Maybe we will start to see more locally grounded solutions, rather than a model that can be replicated everywhere.

So if we're moving toward pluralistic, open, localized possibilities, how then do you define a museum?
FI In my mind, the museum needs to be the place where difficult societal conversations can be held in the widest space possible. It is the museum's responsibility to lead those conversations—not to define the answers, but to be able to address difficult questions.
JL Time is also important. A lot of institutions are reactive and have to shift with the changing of the times. Only a few have the luxury or the structure to engage with a slower time. Museums are among the institutions that can do that.

Nice ideas, but how can a building make space for conversations, to encourage them, catalyze them?
JL Museums have shifted completely compared with the last century. Look at the ratio of gallery space to public space. The share of the museum devoted to public space and amenities has grown, by a lot. That is one clear, specific transformation. Museums also used to be inward-looking. Now, all around the world, they are

trying to turn outward. For Amant, in Brooklyn, we tried to create porosity to bring people deep into the block that the building occupies. These decisions are different from the high-art museum typology of the last century.

FI Another way of putting it is that a building should not be too precious. Basically, you need an un-monumental building.

What frustrates you about the museums you visit? What are your turnoffs?

FI Fear. Fear of bad press. Fear of controversy. You feel it in the organization—the lack of courage. I don't know if that's an architectural problem. It's about the way people govern these structures. During the Black Lives Matter protests, many theaters and cultural spaces opened their lobbies to create rest stations for the protesters. Many museums boarded up their lobbies. That lack of courage is frustrating.

JL My frustration might be a little surprising to you. For me, it's a problem of scale. The more museums grow—and they have grown so much—the harder it is for their administrations to take care of all that space. You often see spaces that are not well considered, not lit well. I find this idea that you must get bigger and bigger, beyond what you can even take care of, very frustrating.

Modes of institutional behavior are encoded into structures. What does museum architecture need to unlearn to achieve greater porosity and inclusiveness?

JL This top-down, single structure that gets bigger and bigger is a problem. What's great about gallery districts like Chelsea in Manhattan is that you have separate entities, and in between them you find urban space. Each organization takes care of its building and tries to be the best it can be. Sometimes I wonder if big museums could operate similarly, with a more urban configuration? Each department could have a level of independence and see itself as a unit in an urban landscape, rather than as part of a top-down structure in which everyone moves in concert.

In Toledo and, for example, the Garage Museum in Moscow, you have such campuses, where life happens between the buildings.

Jing Liu & Florian Idenburg

FI A museum always needs a surface—a wall, a plinth, a floor—that serves as a backdrop against which a curator tells a story. What needs to be unlearned, perhaps, is the way in which stories are told. Galleries can provoke new ways of storytelling. For an early project we did for Z33 House for Contemporary Art, in Hasselt, Belgium (a competition we didn't win), we were thinking of organizing the gallery architecture so that multiple stories could be told simultaneously, maybe even in conflict with one another. Can we allow for contradictory stories to coexist? A lot of this has to do with the relationship between the rooms, and allowing people to narrate their own routes through them.

JL This connects, again, to the size and scale. There was a blip in recent history where everyone was trying to make the largest rooms possible.

FI And there are only maybe four or five artists in the world who have a practice that is able to fill those rooms—and all of those artists are older men.

JL So you end up with the same artists filling up the space with a particular kind of art.

Let's talk about sustainability. How is your thinking evolving about materials and processes museums can use for reducing their ecological footprint?

FI It would be an interesting provocation to question the idea that every museum has to control and maintain and safeguard everything in perpetuity. How do you maintain something stable in an increasingly unstable world? How do you create that buffer between the neutral, perfect, nonchanging gallery or archive and a world that is ever wildering?

At the same time, we think of material and labor as being deeply integrated. For us, a sustainable building practice also means that labor practices should be sustainable. There should always be a clear relationship between what you build and how you build.

JL Typically, the closer labor is deployed to the location, the more equitable it becomes. When the labor is sourced from far away, it tends to be more exploitative. As for materials, since the preservation of cultural heritage is part of the ethos of a museum, we should prioritize materials that need more care. Maybe we can harvest such materials not just from the source, extracted from the earth, but from the existing built environment. We can recycle stones from other buildings and use local labor and technology, so they can be reapplied on a new museum façade. We can give materials multiple lives. Museum buildings do not always need to start from zero.

Is there any justification for new buildings in a world where there are so many existing ones to redevelop?
FI Buildings constructed a hundred years ago might not have been energy-efficient—but they were energy-efficient to build. We are shifting an incredible amount of energy right now to the construction of energy-efficient buildings. The questions extend to museums' international standards, such as those governing the loan of objects. We sometimes work on artist studios, and we see how artworks often move from spaces like garages, where people are smoking and hanging out, into a museum, where the climate has to be perfect. The environments where the work is created and seen are completely different.

So let's get out the crystal ball. The year is 2060. You're visiting a museum with your grandchildren. How different will that museum look and feel?
JL Understanding how it will change requires such a large crystal ball that I'm not even sure I could look into it. But I do believe, like it or not, that people will be in the metaverse within a few decades.
FI I agree. Seventy percent of the US population plays video games. The most successful art exhibition in New York in 2021 was *Van Gogh: The Immersive Experience*. *Proper* museums—highbrow museums—will have to engage with this desire for immersion. Perhaps we will move from a white-cube gallery to a black-box gallery, with more infrastructure for technology.

For now, most digital art spaces look like pixelated Tadao Ando. There is no common design language yet for digital museums.
FI That's the interesting thing. Even in the metaverse, you find ground and walls. But why? You don't need them. KAWS did a show, *NEW FICTION*, in the video game Fortnite, with Serpentine

Jing Liu & Florian Idenburg

Galleries. It looked just like an exhibition in the real world. Why would you re-create physical architecture in virtual space? There is so much space there to think differently.

Let's move from space to time. Time is central to your practice. You have written about how architecture must straddle past, present, and future. Such considerations about temporality seem especially relevant for museums. Am I wrong?

JL It's natural for architects to think about time, because architecture, like the human body, evolves. We already talked about using materials in a more circular way, harvesting them from building sites where they already had a life. That is one tangible way to incorporate time into the material practice of building. I hope our entire industry can move in this direction.

FI We do have to accept some constants. Gravity doesn't change. Materials live on for hundreds of years. Most buildings, by contrast, outlive the functions that they were built to house. A piece of architecture should accommodate a century of ideas, so to speak.

Many types of buildings already house art museums. Show us a department store, a royal palace, a factory, a courthouse, a brewery, a church—we'll take it and we'll turn it into a museum.

JL This also means that we should not be obsessed with pursuing perfect museum typologies. In the past, there was a sense of what was objectively the best layout or proportions for a high-modern art museum. That pursuit is a little bit useless, no? If you're inhabiting a history, then a pure typology has to contend with the idiosyncrasy of history.

Richard Rogers talked about "loose fit" spaces that are able to adapt to future uses. A question I like to ask is: Are we building a screwdriver or a Swiss Army knife? Are we trying to do one thing well, or create a set of tools for doing many things? How does this apply to museums?

FI A clear early example of this principle was the Centre Pompidou, in Paris. Now all around Europe, we find multiple programs being placed in one building. Amant Foundation, the arts complex we designed in Brooklyn, has exhibition spaces, an artist residency, a performance space, a bookshop, a coffee shop, etc. Meanwhile, today's artists are less medium-specific. Spaces such as the Park Avenue Armory, in New York, which can do multiple things at once and merge theater and art, have become much more interesting. By contrast, in many large institutions, you still have arguments over hard lines inside the space—turf wars over what is a gallery and what is not a gallery, and who has jurisdiction. "Is this a corridor? Because if so, it cannot have art in it!"

So if you take this idea of temporality seriously and recognize that buildings will change functions over time, that insight calls for humility. The architect cannot impose her will forever.
FI It's not so much about humility, but about confidence in humanity.
JL It's about understanding your responsibility and place in the larger arc of history. Time is much larger than one architect's life, or one building, or one institution's life. We as architects need to take a more collaborative approach with other temporalities and other cultures. This kind of openness is not a weakness. It takes more confidence to say that we're all part of something larger.

Humility leads us to messages that museums intentionally or unintentionally express. How should a museum make us feel?
JL After practicing architecture for twenty years, you intuitively realize how people perceive materials and geometries. For us, hardcore symmetry is not something we pursue. But we also understand that it cannot just be chaos, and there must be some sense of order. Once you understand order, that order can be softer, and more fluid. And here we find another dimension to materials. Straight architectural spaces are usually built with industrial, mass-produced materials. Curved lines require more craft. We try to make forms that are more enticing and make you wonder what they are.
FI Our entire journey has been about questioning different points of view. A museum should not be there to provide singular answers. Allowing for gaps and different ways of reading and interpretation is important. This doesn't mean that anything goes. We believe in inquiry, scholarship, expertise, and craft. We are not just trying to schlep things together. How do you create

such an open atmosphere? It comes from deep thinking, which manifests itself in the material outcome of our work.

Architecturally speaking, what specifically does it mean to be open or welcoming? How do you actually do it, using your tools?
FI The transition between the street and the gallery is where we can create spaces for discourse, for overlap and friction. Maybe the gallery is stable, but the in-between spaces can allow contemporary conversations to take place.

What about fun? Fun with other people, research has shown, is a key motivator for visiting a museum. Are museums too serious?
JL A 2010 *Wall Street Journal* article about one of our earliest projects, *Pole Dance*, was titled, "A Serious Couple's Fun Project for This Year's PS1 Beach Party." Fun and being serious are not mutually exclusive. In fact, the Bauhaus was very serious about learning and discovering through having fun. Fun might be the most effective way for intelligence to gather more information and evolve. It would be a worthy goal for museums to be a place where people from different cultural backgrounds and social circles can have fun together, like with music or sports, but through visual arts. When we have fun, we are more open to see new things; we are more willing to reach beyond our comfort zones.
FI I do think we can make museums more engaging. One thing we haven't fully mastered yet as architects is the vertical museum. Few have done it better than the Guggenheim Museum in New York. That museum is fun, no? Walking down the spiral is fun. It provides an ever-changing perspective. If Frank Lloyd Wright had provided an opportunity to look out over Central Park here and there, that would be even more fun—or at least more engaging.

Let's return to where we started: the shifting historic context. You have seen a lot already during your careers: the rise of China, a financial crisis, a pandemic, lately the return of superpower conflict. How do you situate museum buildings in this shifting landscape?
JL Maybe I'm only saying this because we're in the middle of a war between Russia and Ukraine, and a lingering pandemic, but I think we're feeling some frustration as architects. As creative

people, we need to be much bolder about where we stand. We can talk about openness and inclusivity and generosity and plurality, but few tangible bold moves have come out of those conversations thus far in our institutions. And there is too much fear of failure. As a society, we're good at criticizing one another. But we need to say, "This idea may not be perfect, but this is where we need to go if we want to face the future." We have to walk the walk. We have been waiting for a paradigm shift since the beginning of our careers. It's been fifteen years. We haven't seen it yet.

Finally, I hear you're building a new office for your practice. How do you design a perfect space to stimulate creativity?
FI We hope it will be a place where people can come together—a place for ideas. We want them to come here at the moments when creative exchange needs to happen. We are defining the size of the office based on a sense of domesticity and intimacy, to create a welcoming space for this exchange.

You may have just described the perfect museum.

Jing Liu & Florian Idenburg

FRIDA ESCOBEDO
Frida Escobedo, Mexico City

SUBTLENESS DOES NOT HAVE
TO BE ORDINARY

I first encountered the Mexico City–based Frida
Escobedo's work in 2018, when she designed a summer
pavilion for the Serpentine Galleries in London. Born
in 1979, she was at that point the youngest-ever recipi-
ent of the commission, which has long functioned as a
kind of reputation accelerator for architects, including
three others in this book. Her structure, which was part
courtyard, part sculpture, and part maze, blurred the
boundaries between inside and outside, new and historic, and global and Mexican design vernaculars. Its
defining feature was a richly textured porosity that lent
the light-dappled pavilion an air of both accessibility
and intrigue. Escobedo's fast-growing practice ranges
from domestic to commercial to institutional. Not long
before our conversation, she was invited to reimagine
the Modern and Contemporary Art wing of The Metropolitan Museum of Art in New York, giving her an
opportunity to implement her ideas about museum
architecture on a whole new scale.

ANDRÁS SZÁNTÓ: *Let's start with Mexico, where you were born and where you started your studio in 2006. What is the unique perspective this part of the world gives you on architecture?*
FRIDA ESCOBEDO: All creative people reflect where they come from, what they have seen, heard, tasted. In my case, I grew up in Mexico City. It's beautiful. It's complex. It's loud, busy, chaotic. Many things need to happen urgently, but sometimes they never do, so people take action and resolve things creatively. That gives it a different expression. The street is where life happens, but indoors you always find a different environment.

It is a city and a country rich in art. The National Museum of Anthropology is one of my favorite museums. What do you take from this context?
We have this idea of layering and metabolizing—of making history part of our present. I am fascinated with spaces that reflect on our history, like El Zócalo, the main square in central Mexico City, where you can see layers of the Aztec city, the colonial city, and the modern city. The National Museum of Anthropology does that layering beautifully. Pedro Ramírez Vázquez was an outstanding architect. He didn't define himself through a style, but rather as someone with a strategy, which was about transforming the past into something that could go into the future, and become a national identity.

That giant canopy at the anthropology museum, a town square in a museum, is right at the cutting edge of contemporary museology.
That's true. He envisioned the museum as not only a space of representation but a space of encounter. That is why the central courtyard is so relevant. It has this grand gesture as you come in, which gives you a splendid welcome with the monumental fountain at the entrance, and as you move into the main courtyard, the water seems to filter out the energy of the street. You are suddenly immersed in a completely different environment, without even noticing it.

I'm curious what other buildings shaped your understanding of what makes a great museum.

I am interested in museums as spaces of encounter, like MASP, in São Paulo, by Lina Bo Bardi. The site had one building condition: It couldn't block the panoramic view of the site. This rule protected what had become an important urban gathering space along Avenida Paulista. Her idea of suspending half of the museum and burying the other half below the terrace level allowed her to keep the plaza space open. Underneath the shade of the gallery spaces, the main plaza remained a place of reunion, celebration, protest, and representation, where everything happens. Paulo Mendes da Rocha did something similar at the Brazilian Museum of Sculpture, also in São Paulo. He designed a massive shade that provides shelter from the sun and rain but also defines the area of the sculpture garden. The museum becomes a sculpture in itself—but an occupiable sculpture.

Another architect in this book, Paula Zasnicoff Cardoso, calls this sort of space a "freedom platform," with roots in Brazilian Modernism and Oscar Niemeyer. Any other architectural philosophies that shaped your thinking about the museum?
A couple of years ago, I received Rémy Zaugg's 1986 book *The Art Museum of My Dreams, or A Place for the Work and the Human Being* as a gift from the gallerist Claes Nordenhake. It contains playful descriptions of what an exhibition space should be like, and how there are certain things that shouldn't really change, such as the conditions of light, or the need for a ninety-degree wall-to-floor angle in order to see artwork that is two-dimensional. I tend to go back to these basic principles, and then I can think with my team about what we could do differently—and that usually has to do with how we relate to other people in the museum.

What attracts you to a museum? What makes it a good space?
This is going to sound like a boring architect's answer, but shifts in scale do keep people engaged with space. You come to a compressed space, and then you encounter a beautiful courtyard or sculpture garden where you can appreciate a monumental work. It is important to have a variety of spaces inside—your favorite little corners, where you can feel like that is your own space;

busy moments for people-watching; others for juxtaposing artworks and creating relationships in your head. Moving from one moment in the history of art to another should not feel like a disconnected journey, but like part of the same experience.

It makes me think of a magazine or a newspaper, this idea of editing together different experiences or ideas.
Or a film. This is also linked to speed. Sometimes you go to a museum just to see two pieces that you love, and you walk quickly, passing through all this other information, and you just focus on those particular pieces. At other times, you can see a whole collection piece by piece. Or you may spend three days coming back to see the same painting. Being able to do all of those things in the same space is important to me. What puts me off are spaces where you cannot make those connections— spaces that are siloed, isolating objects from one another, where there is no possibility of creating this flow in your head.

Each visitor has a multiplicity of motivations. You're a different visitor in the morning than in the afternoon.
Yes, and it's not just that you are not the same person in the morning and the evening; a lot depends on whom you are with and what your relationship to them is. Differentiating yourself from others is how you understand who you are as an individual. Yet your identity is also shaped by belonging to a certain group. Museums are now trying to say, "Even though people are different, we can agree to be different." But certain threads will continue to run through all of us. That is magical. The challenge is that the art on view was often commissioned by specific people at specific moments in history, representing specific ideas. How can we accept that the same object may have different meanings and spark different emotions for different people?

This brings us to porosity. Porosity, along with its sister term transparency, *comes up a lot when architects talk about museums. Tell me what it means to you.*
It means exchange. The possibility of exchange.

A noble idea. Yet instead of porosity, many people who come to a museum feel they are walking into a brick wall, or perhaps a travertine wall. Architecturally speaking, what is a space of open exchange?

As you were describing this travertine wall, the word that came to my mind was *impenetrable*—something that doesn't allow you to get inside, and that does not belong to you. You cannot relate to it. Transparency would be full access, and porosity plays with this duality. There are crevices where you can start getting in, and others that you might recognize as barriers, but they can become more open or more closed. Porosity is a gradient. If you pay close attention, you might realize that you can infiltrate that travertine wall.

Perhaps you mean a kind of pixelation? All those little glimpses add up to some kind of image or understanding, and your job is to make sense of it.

It requires a double responsibility: for the museum to become more permeable, but also for the observer to become more fluid. We need to think about how we can connect to these rather intimidating institutions. Maybe we can connect in a very easy way. That is the difference between transparency and porosity. Porosity is not about trying to provide such an open platform. It requires a bit of work. Once you do that, the relationship becomes richer and more interesting.

But how do we get there? Because, ironically, some of the same high-end design that attracts cultural tourism can also make people feel excluded. How do you navigate this tension?

I think that is changing. A new generation is finding a way to connect with large institutions. Maybe it's because of social media, but younger people seem less fearful. They do want to engage, even if for different reasons. They might just use the museum as a backdrop for their social platforms, for example. They don't seem to have this limitation that "no, this space is not for me." They just go in.

If you look at the flowering of iconic museums since the 1990s, many of the buildings from this period are anything but porous. What is your view?

Frida Escobedo

I agree with you. They are anything but porous. At the same time, they created an attraction. It's almost as if the city became the museum and the museum became an artwork, a sculpture in it. Of course, we are talking about the Guggenheim Bilbao without even having to name it. This idea of transforming a whole city because people want to see an architectural object is quite fascinating to me.

The flip side would be an attitude of restraint or humility. How do you express humility without turning the museum into an ordinary object?
I don't necessarily want to use the word *humble*, but I am thinking about museums that don't have grand gestures—there is no big moment. The Noguchi Museum in New York and the Museo Rufino Tamayo in Mexico City have amazing materiality, but the scale still feels human. You don't feel overwhelmed. I haven't been to the Louisiana in Denmark, but people describe it as having a similar sense of human scale, where the space does not overpower you. Subtleness does not have to be ordinary.

You once said, "Simplicity is complex to achieve." Are some museums overdesigned?
The complexity has more to do with the flow of the spaces than with visual gestures. Yes, I feel some museums are overdesigned, when the shape of the building becomes more important than its contents. Museums are not just containers of art. They are producing cultural content—creating discourse, narratives, connections with artists. If the shape of the space is so strong, there is little room for such mediation. The museum needs to be a facilitator.

If there is one thing that jumps out about your architecture, it's texture. Museums are often full of flatness—drywall, glass, steel, polished stone. Could texture play a bigger role?
It is again more about porosity: playing with light, filtering certain things, unveiling them as you move. It's about how space starts to shift as you move through it. You discover things. My Serpentine Pavilion sometimes looked like a closed box. But if you moved through the space, it started to open up and reveal

the landscape, or someone behind a wall. You would want to move into the next space. Porosity also depends on proximity and scale. Something may not be porous as a whole, but it can have moments of porosity.

Do these ideas reflect a generational shift in the field of architecture? Or am I overstating it?
No, I have the same feeling. The era of the starchitect didn't last too long, and I think that's great. It doesn't mean these weren't absolutely astonishing, memorable buildings. But there has been a shift in the last generation of architects. At some point we realized we don't have that much agency or power, so we would be better as teammates, rather than trying to lead. That is also a way of surviving. Grand gestures depend on a lot of capital, and that is not the only way for architecture to thrive. Perhaps when you cannot do grand gestures or experiment with super-high-tech materials, that creates a potential for our work to actually become more relevant.

We seem to be moving away from the chest-thumping auteur who has a monopoly on what is great art, performance, or literature. We live in a more pluralistic world. It feels outdated to declare that you have the one great idea. With that in mind, how do you define a museum?
It is a space for self-reflection and collective encounter. It acts almost like a collective mirror in which you can see yourself, but also see yourself in relation to others.

But museums are also spaces, and spaces are not neutral; they are full of meanings, innuendos.
A lot of this conversation has been about the front-of-house of the museum. But the back-of-house is also key. The conservation area, where teams work; the storage; the hidden circulation—all that makes the theater of the museum work. Coming back to transparency and porosity, it would be impossible to have full transparency in those areas. But it would be helpful to have a chance to peek, to understand through small glimpses that there is another world in there, the other side of the coin. This would enable you to experience the art you are

seeing, and to recognize that it's not just the curator and the artist who make an exhibition, but a whole range of people.

We may be missing an opportunity for storytelling and creating fascination around the museum. I wonder: How are you think-ing about the trends that will define the future society and the museum in it?
Seeing everything that is happening in the world right now, I can get pessimistic. Instead of becoming more generous and connected, society seems to be becoming more siloed, segre-gated, polarized, and intolerant. This is how I see the future, unfortunately. Is there a way to react to that situation? Would that answer be something that tries to represent all peoples' values? Would it be a space where there can be friction and we can agree to disagree? What is the in-between? Whom are we representing?

The museum is a Western construct—born in Europe, raised in America. But it is being embedded into new contexts around the globe, like Latin America. How might this redefine the museum?
I'm thinking about the Museo Anahuacalli, built by Diego Rivera and covered in volcanic rock, in the south of Mexico City. They recently added a wing by Mauricio Rocha that works with the landscape of the lava fields, including an archive, storage, media labs, and rooms for theater and ballet. It is almost like a cultural hub connected to the landscape. It is successful because it is not just a container for art, but it also creates content while being connected to the landscape and the city—an oasis for a busy neighborhood. It is one of the most successful examples in Latin America of how museums are evolving and transforming into larger things beyond exhi-bition spaces.

Another challenge is to make new kinds of spaces for new forms of art. How do you design for mediated, ephemeral, or yet-to-be-imagined digital practices?
It has to do with being able to mutate flexibly from one shape to another, remaining as open as possible, and understanding what needs to happen inside the doors and what can happen

outside the walls of the museum. That was a big lesson of La Tallera Siqueiros, our project in Cuernavaca, Mexico. It had a very defined perimeter, but just by opening one side of the site we were able to create a connection to the public. It provided an opportunity for performance within the boundary of the museum, actually in its public space.

I am curious about your process. How do you get to the idea? How do you grapple with the tensions we have been discussing?
I tend to listen. That's my thing. I need to understand the client, but I also work in close collaboration with my team. At the studio we are discussing ideas all the time. Everyone has a voice. We all discuss the ideas from the first moment and test them out and see where they take us. To me that is fundamental. Then there is the other side of the conversation, showing the result of that collective effort to the client to see if it reflects what they wanted for the project, and then taking that feedback back to the team. I am almost like a mediator between those worlds.

What about the people who use these structures? How do you listen to them?
That is the biggest challenge. When you are designing a private house, you have one client, and you listen to their needs. I compare designing a public building to playing music. You put your emotions out there and hope someone will empathize with you. It is almost like vertigo—the thrill of not knowing and just throwing yourself out there, because you cannot know if people will respond positively. When they do, it is just magical.

I can't help but bring this up: You are the first woman to design a wing at The Metropolitan Museum of Art, in a profession that is still thoroughly male-dominated. Any reflections?
It continues to be relevant precisely because it hasn't reached the level where we are not asking that question anymore. Until we get to that point, we need to have this conversation about how we create more opportunities for women architects. It's challenging, because it can feel like tokenism. I am wary of that. The real question is, how do we get there? What is the

Frida Escobedo

requirement for women like me to gain trust from people to make more ambitious commissions?

You are working on fascinating projects, from commercial spaces to museums. Meanwhile, the world around us is strained by inequality, polarization, insecurity, war. What is the role and unique power of the museum under these conditions?
In the end, a museum is a space of hope. It's about having hope through beauty, yes, but also knowing that we will persevere and thrive. No matter what, we will be able to transcend.

STEPHAN SCHÜTZ

gmp · von Gerkan, Marg und Partners Architects, Hamburg,
Berlin, Aachen, Beijing, Shanghai, Shenzhen, Hanoi

A LANDSCAPE OF OPPORTUNITIES AND ACTIVITIES

I was introduced to Stephan Schütz in Beijing in 2011, as
he was completing work on the renovation of the National
Museum of China, on Tiananmen Square, directly opposite the Great Hall of the People and steps from Mao's
mausoleum. As a partner in the venerable German architectural firm of von Gerkan, Marg and Partners (gmp),
known for its stadia, airports, and vast infrastructure projects, he was collaborating with a team of architects and
Chinese counterparts on what then was intended to be
the world's largest museum building. It was the culmina-
tion of an ambitious cultural-diplomacy initiative unfolding between Germany and China, and I was writing an
article about the whole endeavor. Since then, Schütz has
continued to conceive and transform museums, concert
halls, and libraries across China and Germany. He brings
to civic architecture the discipline of a Miesian Modernist and a belief that buildings should not overwhelm the
people and functions they serve.

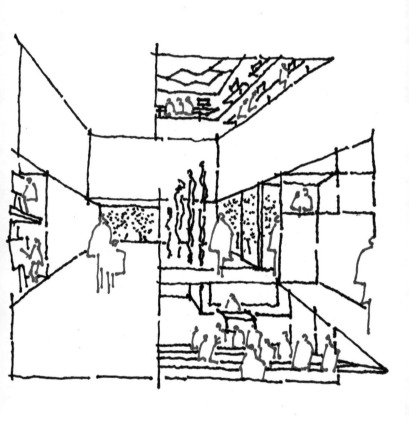

ANDRÁS SZÁNTÓ *We met in Beijing as you were finishing the National Museum of China, in 2011. Right now, as war rages in Ukraine, it's almost strange to be discussing museum architecture.*

STEPHAN SCHÜTZ Indeed, we're far from that time when we first met in Beijing. The world has changed a lot, and things have happened that were unthinkable back then.

The National Museum was intended to be the world's largest museum—yet it was your first museum project. You went straight to the top.

People were asking if we had ever done a museum before we went to work on the biggest museum worldwide. As you can imagine, we struggled with the answer. In the end, through lots of work and having attained a deeper understanding of another culture, we did it. We were then invited to many museum competitions in China. We worked on an exciting museum in Zhuhai; on the China National Arts and Crafts Museum in Beijing, which has a department for intangible art; and on the Museum of the Culture of the Yellow River, which is integrated into the riverside landscape. More recently, we worked with the Staatliche Kunstsammlungen in Dresden on their Japanisches Palais.

What originally formed your perceptions about museums?

When I was a teenager, my parents often took me to the Sprengel Museum, in Hannover. It had all the features I like in museums. It sits by a lake, and there was a kind of artificial landscape—you had to climb a hill overlooking the lake. When you entered, there were lots of different workshop spaces. You had a great view over terraces toward the exhibitions. There was a nice Italian restaurant where we often ate a pizza or pasta after our visits. This was my idea of the museum as a child—a kind of comprehensive experience for a whole day.

That is not a far cry from the kind of experience museums are seeking to provide these days. You live in Berlin now, a city of museums that have served as models for many museums in the past. How does living there color your expectations of museums?

Stephan Schütz

I would like to mention two extraordinary Berlin institutions: the Altes Museum in Lustgarten, designed by Karl Friedrich Schinkel; and the Neue Nationalgalerie by Ludwig Mies van der Rohe, at the Kulturforum. Both have the same intention: to incorporate public space into the museum. They suggest that public space, urban space, and museum should be one.

It goes to show that current discussions about opening up the social and aesthetic functions of the museum are not altogether that new. So how do you define a museum?
The purpose of the museum has changed over the centuries. Nowadays they are less about demonstrating the power of aristocrats, church leaders, and others. What were once private rooms are now open to the public. Warehouses and industrial spaces now serve as museums. In China, and in other places, some museums push the limits of construction; they appear to be artworks. Why is this so? I think many leaders in Chinese cities are striving to construct an identity via major architectural achievements. Is this the right direction for the museum? I wonder.

The past few decades have certainly been a time of look-at-me museums that come across almost as works of art. That notion may have peaked.
For me, these spectacular museum buildings are quite ambiguous. Of course, as architects we are often asked to create a kind of celebrity for the cities we work for. On the other hand, we should also be trustees for our clients. We should not necessarily consume large amounts of public money, which may invite a critical appraisal of our work as architects. Good architecture does not have to be expensive or superficially spectacular.

This hints at your architectural philosophy. I've heard you say that good architecture doesn't need to compete for attention. You come from a tradition of Modernist restraint.
You are absolutely right. Architects don't decide what is going to be built. We decide how to build—a big difference. We decide about space, functions, light, shadow, materials—this is our work. I see us as partners in a dialogue. Good architecture and

good buildings are always the result of a fruitful exchange with all people involved in the process.

You already said that the museum is changing. To keep up with society, what are the key things that museum architects should unlearn?
We must unlearn the idea that a museum is a monofunctional building. It's no longer just a container for art and exhibitions. We have to learn that a museum is first and foremost a place for people. People ought to influence the program of the museum. We need to create spaces for participation—maker spaces, for example. We also have to unlearn the idea that a museum is a pure tourist destination. People are changing attitudes about travel due to the climate crisis. The museum more and more serves the people in the area where it is located.

What other trends shape that future the museum must anticipate?
Orhan Pamuk in *The Museum of Innocence* says that "museums are places where time is transformed into space." People's expectations about that space will change. I think the idea of the Schaulager, an open warehouse museum introduced by Herzog & de Meuron around 2002, will continue to be a major trend. It ties back to the *wunderkammer* of the sixteenth century. It will not replace the white cube, but could exist in parallel with the exhibition space.

When Martin Roth was director of the Victoria & Albert Museum in London, we discussed creating a museum where you could put together your own collection. You would meet some friends, rent space in the museum, and create your own exhibition, which would have been assembled with an automated warehouse system. The visitor would become the curator. Creating more interactive ways to engage with objects may be one future direction that takes us beyond classic, curated exhibition spaces.

Like a karaoke museum. You pick the objects. In Rotterdam the Depot Boijmans Van Beuningen is a radical piece of architecture that questions the protocols of the museum. It asks, "Who's in charge?"

Stephan Schütz

Right. It turns people into more active participants—a people's museum, where the visitors have agency. But if we want to make people engage actively, we need the right spaces for that. We need co-working spaces, more labs. Transparency and openness are not just about see-through walls. They are about allowing different activities, from science to research to administration to education, to be visible in the museum, all at the same time.

So how, ultimately, will tomorrow's museums look and feel?
When you approach the building, you will feel invited. The museum will extend into urban space or nature. Once you enter, you will see lots of different activities: exhibition spaces, work-shops where people are making or restoring artworks. You may see open platforms for education and discussion. You may see researchers and restaurants. It will be a kind of landscape of opportunities and activities. You choose what you want to do. And it will be fun. You should not be obliged to do only what the curators expect you to do.

In Dresden, at the Kulturpalast, we developed an urban living room. On the ground floor we installed a kind of speaker's corner, inspired by the area of Hyde Park in London where anyone can speak up about current issues. Live music is performed there. It's a bit like what the Centre Pompidou tried to accomplish, allowing a mix of functions.

I am curious about your process of designing a museum. How do you get to the big idea?
Normally communication really starts once you win a competi-tion. As I said, a successful project is created out of a dialogue with many people. Our task is to listen to the different groups involved: museum management and staff, engineers, research-ers, planners, authorities. I compare our role to that of a con-ductor guiding different sections of an orchestra. In the end, it should all sound like one entity. This is our work.

This brings us to context. Context, you believe, is everything. Let's start with the international context. As a German Modernist architect who lived for several years in Beijing, how has working overseas changed your ideas about designing?

I have been lucky to work on three major museums in China. These have brought me into new fields of knowledge and understanding. A strong relation to place is the most important to me. This is true of the social and historic context as well. As a consequence of their history, Chinese architects do not identify with the International Style as much as we do. They are asking for more Chinese solutions, for buildings that source their identity from their own traditions or local characteristics.

Most museums are located in cities. How do you think museums should adapt or respond to the cities around them?
If we plan a museum now that will open in ten years, then we have to try to think about what will be happening then. We have to meet the requirements of the future. For example, we are working on the renovation and reconstruction of the Berlin State Library, a fascinating building by the great German architect Hans Scharoun. It is part of the so-called Kulturforum complex, which includes the Neue Nationalgalerie, the Berlin Philharmonie, and soon the Museum of the 20th Century, by Herzog & de Meuron. The conditions of this urban space will change significantly during our planning period. For example, car traffic likely won't play a major role by the time this area is completed. So why can't we think of the Kulturforum as a shared space where pedestrians have priority? We will be connecting museums and other cultural buildings into a better, greener, more silent and sustainable city. The Kulturforum can finally become a real forum.

As a New Yorker, I applaud the idea of a silent city.
With electric vehicles, car noise may no longer be a factor. Now you might buy a ground-floor apartment on a large avenue. Why not? Our attitude toward living in the city may change. Most people won't even own a car anymore. We'll have shared mobility services. So we won't need as many parking lots. What then could we do instead with the spaces in front of museums? They could become sports fields, theaters, or playgrounds. We should consider this when we envision the future of museums in a future city.

Stephan Schütz

You're saying that if you tie a museum too closely to its present context, you risk its becoming outdated?

We should provide space for whatever might happen in the future. What we now call a "museum" may eventually house something completely different. That is why flexibility is key if we want to create spaces with a long-lasting future. At the same time, wherever possible we should use existing buildings and transform them. A major trend in the future will be to preserve so-called "gray energy"—energy going into the production, transport, and storage of materials.

Much of the current discussion around museums is about providing space for the community. Can museums live up to that? Most museums today don't feel like especially welcoming community spaces.

The idea of a cultural center that houses spaces for music, exhibitions, restaurants, libraries, in one single building or group of buildings might be one way forward for museums. This was already a trend in the past—think of the Barbican Centre in London, which opened in 1982, or Lincoln Center in New York, which opened in 1962. The Centre Pompidou is one of the best examples. It's so much more than a museum. We can revisit these cultural complexes. But there are even bigger possibilities.

Not long ago, we were invited to join other architects to think about the future of JFK International Airport, in New York. We came to the conclusion that a museum for the people waiting at the airport might be a good idea. We should think about how the function of the museum may be combined with other purposes. Why can't the museum be part of a hospital complex, for example, where people stay for days and weeks?

Some museum designs are essentially shells, and then a different design team takes over for the interior program. Elsewhere, the architect designs the entire experience. Where should the architect's control end?

If you're asking me, the answer will be that our work should start with urban design and end with organizing an exhibition—at least one. I strongly recommend that our clients let us think about the building from the shell to the interior, in order to make sure that our design accommodates all the details.

I personally find a lot of exhibition design to be quite formulaic and repetitive.
The more an exhibition is focused on a particular subject or message, the better it is in my eyes. And exhibition design should aim to make visitors think, rather than just entertain them.

Here's a technical question: How do you think about lighting the galleries?
Light is invisible. What we perceive is reflections on surfaces. And light also means shadow. Here's my philosophy: I like to enhance the importance of particular architectural elements and reduce the importance of others with lighting concepts. The overall target is to create a strong perception of space. Daylight and artificial light are completely different. It is hard to make them coexist, because daylight is two hundred times more intense than artificial light. And it is dynamic; it changes throughout the day. Therefore, we pay close attention to where we use daylight and where we use artificial light in a museum.

Many painters work with northern light in their studios. This is the reason why we use the same daylight source for galleries. But still, daylight is quite critical due to its nonconstant intensity and high UV content. For this reason, LED lighting, with its brilliant color rendering, will play an increasingly important role in future museum planning.

Thinking about that blank white wall, the white cube has been the defining architectural space for art since the mid-twentieth century. I often say the white cube is a period room. It represents a certain ideal about art from a certain time. What is its future?
It will somehow coexist with new forms of exhibition space. In terms of flexibility, it seems to offer perfect conditions for exhibition organizers. But you can easily get tired in these kinds of galleries. And we know that white walls are completely unsuitable for many works of art.

I would like to dig deeper into the mood of museums. As you mentioned, museums are often quite institutional in an older sense: stone, glass, hard benches—super-serious. How should a museum feel?

Stephan Schütz

It should feel like a living room for many people. This is what I experienced at the Isabella Stewart Gardner Museum, in Boston, which impressed me a lot. You feel you are being invited into this house, with plants and a living room with comfortable sofas instead of hard benches. However, it is important that a museum feel different from a commercial space. There is comfortable seating in a Starbucks, but a museum shouldn't feel like a Starbucks. There should be internet, but the data should be safe. I imagine it as a comfortable space, a green space, a transparent space, open to the city and vice versa. Museums, as public institutions, could serve as role models for other buildings.

The truth is that many people are put off by art museums. Architecturally speaking, how do you signal openness without turning the building into something too quotidian?
We should strive for a timeless architecture with people-friendly and sublime spaces. People will feel this generosity. You are free to stroll around and make your own decisions. There should be interactive areas where you can have fun, and other places where you feel concentrated and focused. A good museum is built on contrasts: dark and bright, spiritual and playful, natural spaces and aesthetic architecture. A place where life unfolds in many different ways—without obligation, and with no commercial interest. A museum should make people curious to see what's inside. Then we are on the right track.

Finally, what is it that you wish you had known when you set out to work on one of the world's largest museums, something you know today and would want every museum architect to know?
Today, of course, I see the shortcomings, and we have mentioned them—the hard benches, the stone walls, the heavy focus on exhibitions and objects. Looking back, I might suggest a mixing of functions. With everything we have learned over the past fifteen years, I might focus more on the comfort of the visitors, to create a more active and self-determined experience of the museum.

LINA GHOTMEH
Lina Ghotmeh – Architecture, Paris

A PLACE OF FREEDOM

What does it mean for a museum to be a site of
living memory? This question underlies the work
of Paris-based Lina Ghotmeh, a designer of richly
textured cultural and domestic spaces. Born and raised
in war-torn Lebanon, Ghotmeh takes an archaeological approach to museum-making that both exposes
and helps overcome acrimonious histories. Case in
point: her Estonian National Museum in Tartu, built
on a decommissioned Soviet airfield, where people are
not only reminded of the painful past but also invited
to activate new communal experiences underneath a
massive canopy. For Ghotmeh, museum architecture
must incorporate a profound understanding of the
history in which it is situated. But it also demands a
fresh vocabulary of empathy, generosity, and sensitivity
that prioritizes the comfort and agency of the visitor.
In her methodology, a reckoning with the past—including the legacy of the museum—paves the way to a
brighter future.

ANDRÁS SZÁNTÓ *"An archaeology of the future" is how you*
have sometimes described your research-driven practice. Can you
tell me where that idea comes from?

LINA GHOTMEH It is related to growing up in Beirut, a city
that lived through terrible wars but is also the cradle of many
civilizations. Earthquakes have buried Beirut more than seven
times. Whenever you dig, you uncover a link to a past civilization. I was always drawn to narrating history through the
rediscovery of artifacts. For me, having grown up in a devas-
tated city, architecture is a way of relating back to earth, to what
lies beneath. Architecture should have the capacity to heal a
landscape, to bring people back together. This is where I started
to develop an architecture that echoes archaeology.

We are on day 170 of the war in Ukraine. In 2018 you did a compe-
tition proposal for the Museum of Revolution of Dignity, in Kyiv.
I am curious, given what we are living though, how you think
about it today.

They wanted to mark a moment in their history—the revolution in Maidan Square—through a museum: a commemorative
structure that would function as an active institution. It would
stand on the top of a hill, connected by a long street to Maidan
Square. It would not just be a container of artifacts of the revolution—the rubble, the bottles they threw, etc.—but a place
where people could meet and where dialogue could happen for
a culture to be perpetuated.

   This project raises for me the question of museums as
"memorials," and how they could operate as more active ones.
They do contain archaeologies of the past, but they can also
play a crucial role in activating our present and foreseeing our
future. That is, in some way, what I mean by an archaeology of
the future.

The same aspiration is reflected in your Estonian National
Museum, a poetic structure with its long form and huge canopy.

The site in Tartu is adjacent to an ex-Soviet military airfield, one
of the largest in the Baltic states, a bearer of undesirable memories for Estonians. The runway cuts through the landscape. It
just sits there, untouched, a palimpsest of this painful history.

In my mind, on this site the museum couldn't simply sit as an icon, indifferent to these traces on the ground. Its architecture had a responsibility to initiate a new dialogue and a new kind of space.

Having grown up in Beirut, I saw a great opportunity here to conciliate people with the history of a place through a unique architecture. As such, the building shape emerges in continuation to the airfield, allowing the museum to gain a territorial scale. The building delves into the landscape on which it sits. It offers, foremost, a platform where people can meet and narrate their past, live their present, and build their future. Its spaces are a cultural incubator for the Estonian population.

Before starting your own practice, in 2006, you had collaborated with Jean Nouvel and Foster + Partners. Was it then that you formed your ideas about designing museums?
I wouldn't say that I shaped my ideas there. Constructing concepts or making architecture is a continuous and lengthy process. Surely it was instructive to work with Jean Nouvel for two years and a half (including an experience at Foster, for a joint venture Nouvel had with him). But my understanding of museums was born out of my now twenty years of practice, starting with the Estonian Museum and followed by other museums I designed for art collectors, designs for exhibitions, and so on.

My education at the American University of Beirut gave me a multidisciplinary perspective on architecture. I was interested in other fields, such as sociology, anthropology, biology; these were part of my architectural education. Museums are multidisciplinary realms where an architect should question the status quo and seek newness. I see museum architecture as a porous one, creating open structures that are actively vocal and critical about history, memory, people, society, objects.

What does the museum symbolize in the context of Lebanon's contested history?
In Lebanon, the absence of governmental structures makes the museum an essential realm for the public. It is a place of togetherness and a diversity of cultures and religions. Museums

can be ambassadors to the world, where everyone can feel an intrinsic belonging and freedom to be.

A few years ago, we designed a museum of modern art in Beirut, for a competition. The site was going to be right on the historic Green Line separating East and West Beirut. To me the museum had to contain, through its architecture, the history of its particular site. While it would sit on a boundary, what used to be an immaterial "wall" separating the city, it would emerge now as a spire, a porous front. I conceived the museum as an "open wall" rising up in the skies of Beirut. It would manifest itself as an open agora, the whole experience orchestrated through a continuous promenade via a ramp unfolding from the ground toward the heights of the city. This would be a place where performances could happen and people could gather in a safe place, looking out over the city.

The Middle East has been a growth area for museums recently. What have these projects brought to the region?
You may say the pyramid was an ancestor of the museum. It was a creation and perpetuation of the culture itself. It was rooted as well in traditional construction techniques and knowledge systems. The contemporary museums mushrooming lately in the Middle East, by contrast, lack that profound connectedness. We see a Western model imported into the region. I would be curious to experiment with a distinctly Middle Eastern museum. That typology has yet to be invented.

You are based in Paris, a city of museums. Many architects of your generation were influenced by the Centre Pompidou. I wonder if that is the case for you?
Centre Pompidou is timeless. It responded to the zeitgeist of its time, and yet it remains contemporary. It has this wonderful porosity. It is connected to the city, constantly active through the plaza in the front, and by virtue of how the space inside can be used in a flexible way.

What other museums do you see pointing the way forward?
Another museum that touched me is the Louisiana Museum in Denmark, especially how it reveals the capacity of the museum

Lina Ghotmeh

to not be stagnant, and how it was and continues to be built incrementally. SANAA's Louvre-Lens has a strong poetic experience that I appreciate.

Given all this, how would you define a museum?
I am critical about the museum turning into a place of consumption, where you merely consume art and objects. For me, the museum must be a place of freedom where one can question society, reinvent, innovate. A place of work and pleasure, where artists can dwell—a kind of polymorphous structure, not just a container. A place where one can exit from daily life and construct a new mindset. One would perhaps spend a few days there. Whilst we may be going into a more digital direction, I tend to think museums should remain places where materiality is very much present, even if combined with a digital, immaterial experience.

You have designed apartment buildings, restaurants, boutiques, offices. What makes a museum different?
I approach even an apartment building with a museum mindset. I'm always thinking about how the building can express the site's history, how it could make people live differently, involve a more diverse range of functions, and be a place of serendipity. The difference is that a museum client already wants an extraordinary building, while an architect has to fight to elevate more "mundane" typologies.

I am curious what you like and dislike about the museums you visit? What frustrates you about them?
The austerity and neutrality of the spaces. This white-cube fashion is, of course, about a desire to relate to an object. But it is too pristine. It also reveals the socioeconomic and political underpinnings of such institutions. In addition, I am often frustrated by the lack of available information. I want to learn more. I would like more human interaction. An artifact is never stagnant—we build meaning around it. Being able to discuss and possibly question the work is precious. Galleries as a spatial structure usually do not support this iterative interaction.

So how then could tomorrow's museums look and feel different?
This question makes me think of the Saradar Collection Open
Storage we designed in Lebanon, where we developed a new
approach to collection display, configured to enable instanta-
neously evolving exhibitions. Visitors are the actual curators
here, as they enter directly into the archives, opening drawers,
unfolding the collection. One can experience a multiplicity of
narratives as the collection is uncovered. We shied away from
the idea of the singular piece sanctified on a wall. It is important to be aware that how we display or select art echoes our perception of dominant cultures and reflects on how we construct
our society.

*The archive museum certainly represents a new step in empower-
ing the visitor. Let's dig a little deeper into this idea of the archaeology of the future and the research that must go into a building.
Can you describe your process?*
It has to start with a question. We must ask, "What is a
museum?" We would go through the history of this typology,
back to the *museion*, this place of learning devoid of collection
per se and dedicated to learning, to the arts. Through this
archaeological process, we try to understand how the typology of the museum has shifted from a particular geographic
place—thinking about Ennigaldi-Nanna's museum in the Neo-
Babylonian Empire in Iraq, or the Pyramids, as the earliest form
of a "collection"—to the emergence of cabinets of curiosity in
eighteenth-century Europe, where the wealthy would gather
assortments of curious artifacts. That typology would spread
around the world before giving way to a more dominant institution, the public museum, with the birth of the Louvre in France.

This research-driven approach allows me, as an architect,
to be rooted in the redevelopment of the museum typology,
to understand its intimate relationship with the culture and
the economic systems that produce it. It allows me to take a
more critical approach to the type of museum I would envision.
Of course, this archaeology is brought in parallel with other
ones, including a thorough understanding of the physical
site, the climate, the environment, the geology, the social
construct of a place. This is not a linear process, but a constant

Lina Ghotmeh

intersection of fields that generate enough density at some point to become a project.

How important is following the program versus following your own understanding of what is best?
I rarely follow a program blindly. I always try to question it, knowing that it is rooted in preconceptions about how things should be. That does not mean that I ignore the needs underlying the program of a building, nor the need for the space to be usable and functional. It is about establishing new relationships and allowing for this new immaterial added value through the act of making.

There is a philosophical question lurking in here about what is really new. Is the new something that has never been seen? Or is it revealed from what is already there, and you lead us to it?
I do think it is about a deep understanding and reinvention of what is already in front of us. Otherwise one may fall into the superfluous. You should not throw out or waste what you already have. Instead, let's think more in depth about what we have, and figure out a way to give it more relevance, more robustness, recomposing the elements adjusted to the needs of the moment.

These days, it seems, museum architects are in a bind. They seek to move forward from look-at-me architecture to one of porosity and embeddedness. But they don't want to make the museum feel ordinary, either. How do you navigate this tension?
You have to make beauty accessible to everyone. Museums are places where you can excel because you are given the means to excel. Therefore, we shouldn't try to make them look mundane. They should be places where we can push the limits and make the ordinary sublime. Yet they must be integrated into society, where everyone feels at ease, not merely spaces for the elite.

Opening up the museum in this way is a challenge, both institutionally and architecturally. How do you design for those outcomes?
The first thing that comes to mind is the image of people queuing to get into that museum temple, through a single door.

That already contradicts the idea of the museum as a porous structure. Architecturally, you should perhaps be able to get in through multiple points, and each point could introduce a new functionality. The challenge for the museum is to become more tentacular and polymorphic, even in its management system, which need not be hierarchical, nor comprised of a homogeneous typology of people.

How much of this is about rethinking the ratio of exhibition to community space?
We definitely need more community spaces in museums. But I wonder about the exhibition space typologies too. Should they still operate like a classic gallery, where you see objects in a rather linear fashion, or more like an open archive or an immersive experience?

Exhibitions, too, may have to change. We could alternate between dense places with objects and spaces where you are immersed in a digital world. Museums should become places where you can experience heightened emotions in relation to the environment and to your body. They are not only containers of objects, but spaces of experience, of learning, and of emotions that can operate without any object at all.

How should such a space of experience and emotions feel?
Very intimate. It could create a moment of humanity, of intimacy, safety. More accessible. More humane. Less institutional. Museums should allow you to evolve as a human being, in your relationship to the world.

So many museums are the opposite, if we're honest. We know what people think of as welcoming and comfortable. We see it in hotels and apartments. Why isn't more of that seeping into museums?
Because of this desire to express the idea that the museum should last forever, like a tomb, a mausoleum for artworks. Maybe we can make the museum a more experimental place for material innovation. We are increasingly going back to vernacular methods of construction, with biosourced, low-carbon-impact materials. We are looking into brick, wood, stone, even

Lina Ghotmeh

3D-printed earth construction. We seem to be coming back to building with more intimate and natural materials that resemble nature, and as such, us as humans.

What does sustainability mean for you in this context? Is it even acceptable to build these big new buildings at all?
Museums do consume a lot of energy, especially if they have a collection that requires a constant level of temperature and humidity. We are now starting to use porous materials that allow us to loosen humidity controls. We are thinking about how museums could produce their own energy. Museums can't just be these big monsters sitting in a place eating up energy.

We are currently designing a manufacture for Hermès. Of course, a manufacturing facility uses a lot of energy. Yet we are designing this building to be a passive low-carbon building, and it turns out that it is totally feasible to build a factory using bioclimatic methods of design complemented with green energy. If such commercial typologies can do it, museums can do it, too.

I wonder what you think of the museum as a place for healing. Your projects in Kyiv and Lebanon address traumatized communities in need of repair. Can architecture nurture moments of solace?
With my students at Yale and in Toronto, we recently developed a studio that focuses on post-traumatic landscapes. We concluded that after a trauma, people need to come together, and community spaces become more crucial. You need places where people can share pain and take time to understand what happened—like an injury in a body that needs time to heal. Museums could be par excellence places for togetherness, so communities could talk about their traumas and come to terms with what happened in their history.

You are a woman in a male-dominated profession. Any thoughts about that?
I don't know if it's about being a woman or not, but I do feel that our built environment is a patriarchal one. It is not inclusive enough in terms of biodiversity and cultural diversity. We are surrounded by "icons," and likewise the current museum

trend is still about icons dominating their surroundings. Control is ever-present in the planning of our cities. Nature is constantly tamed. I think we need more agility, more uncertainty and surprise, more porosity between our built spaces, between our cities and nature. In short, what we need is more *lack* of control.

Lack of control leads us back to our moment. The city where you grew up is on the brink. Societies are polarized. The climate crisis is looming. What gives you hope about what you can achieve with your tools, especially as a museum architect?
Museums can help us think about the power of togetherness. They allow us to have the desire—and the pleasure, actually—of going on with life. You need that desire. You need that pleasure. They help us see that we have gone through a lot, and in turn realize how we can transform our present into a better future.

MINSUK CHO
Mass Studies, Seoul

THE MUSEUM AS A PLAYGROUND FOR ALL

Asia has been the most fertile breeding ground for museums in the twenty-first century. But social and cultural arrangements vary markedly across the vast continent. Having evolved into the world's eleventh-largest economy, the Republic of Korea is becoming an international cultural hub. Its vibrant democracy and systemic investments in education and civic life have made the small East Asian nation especially welcoming for new arts venues. Among the architects driving this institutional efflorescence is Minsuk Cho, founder of the Seoul-based Mass Studies. Born in 1966, Min, as he is called, is part of a generation that has shaped South Korea's spectacular urban and cultural transformation. His exhibition spaces, now numbering around thirty, range from offbeat facilities for grassroots initiatives to polished commercial art galleries to full-scale public museums. His largest project to date involves the repurposing of a decommissioned power plant into a sprawling multi-use cultural center—Seoul's answer to the Tate Modern.

MUSEUM AS A PLAYGROUND FOR ALL

2022. 8   MINSUK CHO

ANDRÁS SZÁNTÓ *We overlapped at Columbia University in the late 1980s and early 1990s. You went on to work for James Polshek and OMA, Rem Koolhaas's office. What influences have those experiences left on you?*

MINSUK CHO I was part of the earlier generation of what became an exodus avalanche of young Koreans all over the world. Columbia at the time was one of the most exciting architecture schools, for its diversity of scholars and practitioners. It was a year after the 1988 *Deconstructivist Architecture* show at The Museum of Modern Art. Rem Koolhaas and Frank Gehry gave lectures there, and Bernard Tschumi was dean. I was hardly able to understand English, but I had an ambition to absorb everything. I met two of my greatest teachers, Richard Plunz, a scholar of New York City urban history, and Kenneth Frampton, who has been a guiding figure in my life.

Polshek was also a great teacher. He played an important role nurturing the cultural sphere in New York, for example with the Hayden Planetarium at the American Museum of Natural History, one of my last projects with him. Rem's office found me because they had projects in Korea, including the Leeum, Samsung Museum of Art and others. From 1996, I started going back regularly from the Rotterdam office to Seoul, and I ended up absorbing the beginnings of a contemporary art scene in South Korea. By then the Gwangju Biennale had launched, one result of the new democracy that emerged from the civic movement.

You established your studio in Seoul, Mass Studies, in 2003, using a name found in both science and sociology. Can you elaborate?
Precisely. The word *mass* interests me because architecture is an intersection of many disciplines. Our goal is to serve society in various roles, by learning from it.

You are operating in a vibrant East Asian economy. The art and museum scene in Seoul seems to be booming these days.
The history of the museum here is relatively short. Museums started in eighteenth-century Europe, initially as private and aristocratic spaces that eventually became more public. Americans made everything more systemic and somehow developed this big international standard in the twentieth century. In

Korea, unlike in other regions, the museum was not tied to an imperialistic history. South Korea went through a compressed period of democratization over the past three decades and entered a super-global, neoliberal arrangement. Art is a stronger focus now and, unlike in the past, less likely to be used for state propaganda. It is part of civil society. Museums and cultural institutions came out of that roller coaster of social change.

It seems to be a golden age for art and culture. And you have been at the center of it. You worked on the Pace Gallery, the Songwon Art Center, Space K. Is there a common element?
We have made almost thirty exhibition-space-type projects, and each one is unique. One early commission was a city initiative, originally a film gallery in a six-meter wide, seventy-meter stretch of underused subway passage assigned to an organization run by a group of young, twenty-something independent filmmakers. However, they didn't want a mere passive display of old movie posters along the subway passage. They ambitiously wanted an indie-film-festival venue, and an education program and other elements, along with exhibition walls. They called it the Chungmuro Intermedia Playground. It is interesting to think about the museum as a playground for all.

Another inventive project was spearheaded by Sunjung Kim, who ran the Gwangju Biennale from 2017 to 2021. She was overseeing the archive and research center of the Asia Cultural Center in Gwangju, a huge, airport-size—maybe too oversized—complex. She came up with "Library Park," a museum-plus-library concept. On one side there was a 200-meter-long gallery exploring thirty different themes, and right next to it a library in the same length with corresponding books. It reminded me of Bernard Tschumi's term from the '90s, *transprogramming*—the idea of combining two functions that are not usually combined. We did a project for a rather humble art storage for a contempo-rary art collector, Ssamzie, that is open for public showings of a regularly changing program of curated, unpacked works. We did a house museum for a collector who lived alone with her dog and a lot of art. You name it. A museum space does not need to be rigid. It can integrate many disciplines and aspects of life.

*These early experiments seem to have been a warm-up for
your Danginri Power Plant complex, Seoul's answer to the
Tate Modern. Can you briefly describe it?*

The project has been discussed since 2004, and over five
changes in government it has continued because the location
has such power. The area used to be at the margins of Seoul,
but now it is quite central. The Han River runs by it. The river is
more than a kilometer wide, but it is more or less walled in by a
highway and high-rise apartment blocks. The Power Plant may
be a last chance to create vibrant riverfront activity that is cultural. The Tate Modern's globally viral influence—reusing old
structures—is obvious. For me, it is a rare opportunity to create
a widely used public space that is so needed here.

We wanted something that you cannot replicate anywhere
else. Lina Bo Bardi's MASP, in São Paulo, is an inspiration,
with its iconic open plaza. Another inspiration is SESC
Pompéia Factory, also in São Paulo, and one of Lina Bo
Bardi's best works. I went to Brazil on a pilgrimage to see her
buildings. At SESC, an industrial building had been turned
into a library and exhibition space with a theater. My friend
told me I should go for lunch. It was a most inspiring sight.
There was a huge hall with a canteen, and people from all walks
of life were there, from grandparents to children to hipsters.
It felt utopian.

Lina Bo Bardi's later structures for SESC were a sports and
recreation facility, with a swimming pool and basketball court.
This can be an altogether inspiring model. Civic spaces should
not be places you visit once or twice a year. You should be able
to go there on a walk and bring your dog. Humans are living
longer now, so civic spaces have to engage various generations
with various activities.

*The Power Plant is not a typical building for Seoul. There is
something perhaps too precious about Korean and Japanese
architecture, with its poetic minimalism. Here you seem to
appreciate a certain rawness that is more in keeping with contemporary urban life.*

We have to do it all. We do need small, exquisite buildings in
certain contexts—acupuncture points, so to speak. At the same

time, embracing roughness is relatively new for us. It comes from a new way of thinking about the city, as Seoul's population has stopped growing in the past two decades.

When people ask about my favorite museums, the Leeum, Samsung Museum of Art is always near the top of my list. You worked on it early on. Which other museums are your icons?
I like some classic museums, like the Museo Nacional del Prado in Madrid, which is mind-blowing, mainly because of the art and the aura of the old building. Museo Tamayo, in Mexico City, is a great museum. It is refreshing that it is not a white-box museum, with so much architectural specificity, while the rest of the world was copying the American white-box model. Architecture and art challenge each other in a wonderful way.

How do you define a museum?
It is where everyone can be comfortable by themselves and express themselves creatively, while being kind to each other—which is the basis of civility. The internet gave us a false hope that it would enable lateral and open exchange. But it has turned into a manipulative algorithm ghetto, as we know. We need a truly civic space, and we need to define that space. The museum has potential to present a polyphony of ideas and allow people to learn from one another. Architecture can create specific and powerful experiences for that to happen, using space, sound, taste, and nonverbal communication—experiences that are not downloadable.

Much of your practice is devoted to civic spaces, public infrastructure, such as parks and even religious buildings. What have you learned from them?
We look for two things. One is static spaces, and the other is fluid space that connects them. There is, of course, a full spectrum between these two. You need to control these flows to then arrive, at a certain point, at a place that lifts people up. At the same time, you need to create a feeling like you are in a living room, even if you are with a hundred other people, which I call "collective intimacy." Everyone should feel at home. What

architects can do is design the space to feel truly inviting and generous, so everyone can feel they belong.

But how exactly? When I think of, let's say, what makes a good restaurant, I know the answer.
Well, good food, first.

Yes, certainly. But also low light, soft chairs, low sound; we know the design language. I am curious what makes a civic space, architecturally? What's the magic that makes it feel like it's for everybody?
Since you made a restaurant analogy, let me tell you a story. One day I was eating in my favorite restaurant in Gwangju, in an old, traditional house. I asked the owner if she would ever open a branch in Seoul. For her that was unthinkable, because so much of what they do is tied to their location. They grow and ferment what they cook right in their backyard; that is part of the restaurant's long history. Civic buildings likewise have to have a strong sense of being rooted in a place. Time completes architecture, in a way. This is why, to me, the museum as instant icon is over. More and more, I find there are better ways to do architecture.

It does seem like the current generation is rejecting the big-time-iconic-architecture approach.
I have to be a bit diplomatic, but when you consider these amazing-looking buildings, you also have to look at the regions that allowed them to happen. During this era of the iconic buildings, questions about context and how it performs have been willfully ignored, in a way.

Do you believe architecture can promote civic virtues, like empathy, participation, solidarity? Does architecture have a capacity for that?
Not by itself. It plays a role as a tool or apparatus, to demonstrate something and engage people, or uplift their spirit. But ultimately, it's just a hardware. You need the right software— and that's why architects need good clients.

Let's stay on politics for a moment. Some believe a museum should engage head-on the social and political realities around it. Others believe it should stand apart, as an oasis, a sanctuary, a place where you can run away. Where do you stand?

It's not an either-or. I go back to Korean film. You have probably seen the 2019 movie *Parasite*, by Bong Joon-ho. What gave him this distinctive voice was his ability to synthesize the escapist blockbuster genre with sharp social critique. The museum is a bit like that. The dichotomy of the serious, confrontational, important stuff versus the seemingly non-political, engaging, and delightful can be resolved. Great art can achieve both at the same time.

Great art can somehow merge these together, yes, but in a building you have physical constraints. A space where I am engaging with harsh questions is not necessarily the space where I can have a beautiful, introspective moment.

Engagement versus escape—I think you can do both. Big museums mix programs like that intentionally. In a smaller case, at Space K, which we designed recently, they have started regular yoga programs in the gallery space. In front of giant, gory, bloody paintings by a young Korean painter, you have thirty beautiful women in Lululemon outfits doing yoga. I don't know how exactly to think about this slightly absurd sight. Yet it is an interesting clash, and a positive one, hopefully. You need to experiment with a whole spectrum of ways to engage.

What are some of the things that frustrate you about museums?

Actually, there are so many. In Korea, my most recent complaint is about overdesigned exhibitions. I get annoyed. The urge to overdesign is encouraged by digital culture, such as Instagram. Laziness is a problem also—the laziness of not taking a keen interest in everything around you.

You live in a city that has grown fifty-fold in one century. How can museum buildings anticipate change and find ways to make sense in that future?

If museums were to develop the way I would like, they would further promote diversity and diverse ways of engagement. The

Minsuk Cho

museum has been treated almost like a luxury good, which is a huge missed opportunity. It should engage the entire ecology of a city and the natural world. When I compare the museums I visited in the 1980s and 1990s to today's, I find that few things have really changed that much, other than their getting supersized. I hope museums will become more participatory, more of a civic platform or playground for learning new things. Instead of going to school, you will go to museums for an immersive environment where you might be able to participate in a less committed but more intensely focused and fluid way. I think there will be more demand for that, as we will live longer, having to learn constantly about the changing world.

What is your way of designing a museum? And how important is following the brief versus following your own understanding of what is best?
It's a combination of discoveries and inventions, depending on the context. Sometimes the conditions given are good enough just to highlight the potentials, as with the Power Plant. Sometimes you start with a clean slate, as with Space K, where the urban substance around it did not exist ten years ago. And usually it is based on a great negotiation with the client. For Space K, they wanted three exhibition spaces with different ceiling heights. We proposed a giant sloping roof that goes from eleven feet to forty feet tall, with all three spaces combined under one concrete shell, using temporary walls. We told them, "You can use this for decades, even a hundred years—who knows how art will change." That is what architects do. I was not trying to be different for difference's sake, or to rebel. In the end, they agreed that it would be great to have one giant, adaptable space where many kinds of project can happen in the future.

We have been talking about civic architecture and how it serves people. Can they have a voice in the design process?
I think so, but not in order to have a populist decision. I have done presentations for five hundred citizens interested in a project. It was almost like being on a reality show. Nowadays in

competitions, often there are around five jurors, and one vote represents the public. I think this is a good conversation to have.

I want to come back to the museum as a playground, which evokes the ideas of Cedric Price. Your Power Plant is modeled on his Fun Palace in some ways. As an architect, how are you thinking about balancing people's thirst to be entertained with a seriousness of purpose?

The Power Plant is a "found" fun palace, and I am interested in serious fun. Lina Bo Bardi's SESC successfully engages the general public, but the performances and exhibitions were nonetheless quite serious, from what I saw at the time. I am not saying museums should be elitist, but I do think specific voices need to be heard, even when what they have to say may not seem popular. We are saturated already with entertainment venues that call themselves museums. The Trick Eye Museum, part of an international chain, has been the number-one most visited "museum" in Seoul. We in South Korea practically invented the Instagrammable museum. We have not been shy about throwing stuff into a building and calling it a museum. But in the end, we have to draw a line; otherwise it's ridiculous.

I would like to conclude on the role of the architect in today's world. As society changes, museums are rethinking their priorities. How do you see your role in this shifting context, given your interest in designing spaces for civic communities?

The architect is not a magical problem-solver. We are not a mighty God, opening up a box that hid the great gift of our genius. Neither are we doctors who write prescriptions for problems. Artificial intelligence will provide such specialized knowledge in the future, using algorithms and data, and it will do a better job. What will survive are not doctors but nurses. Nurses spend more time with patients. That need will always remain, because nurturing is something only humans can do. Architecture, likewise, is not about a single brilliant moment—boom, you reveal an idea and you leave. You have to be anchored to a specific place, and one project alone can take years, or even a lifetime. The important thing is to collaborate with people along the way. That is the essential role of an architect.

You are getting many commissions now, including for museums. What is it that you now know about designing arts spaces that you wish you had known at the start of your career?
Early on in my career I felt compelled to show everything I could do with each project. I have to say, I was overambitious, trying to preach more than to listen, to prove what I could do. Now I have more experience. And I hope I am a better listener.

DAVID ADJAYE
Adjaye Associates

Rendering of Edo Museum of West African Art (EMOWAA), Benin City, Nigeria. View from entry pavilion showcasing sculpture garden and glimpses into entry lobby, education spaces, and contemporary art galleries on the ground level.

National Museum of African American History and Culture, Washington, D.C.

PAULA ZASNICOFF CARDOSO
& CARLOS ALBERTO MACIEL
Arquitetos Associados

Rendering of Contemporary Pinacoteca, São Paulo

Education Center (top) and Claudia Andujar Gallery (bottom) at Inhotim, Brumandinho, Brazil

BJARKE INGELS
BIG | Bjarke Ingels Group

Musée Atelier Audemars Piguet, Vallée de Joux, Switzerland

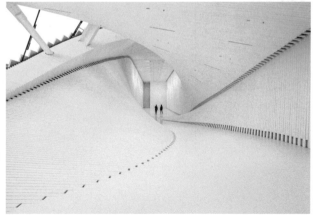

The Twist Museum, Jevnaker, Norway

KABAGE KARANJA & STELLA MUTEGI
Cave_bureau

Installation view of *The Anthropocene Museum: Exhibit 3.0 Obsidian Rain*, 2017, at the 17th International Architecture Exhibition – La Biennale di Venezia

Renderings of proposed Cow Corridors, Nairobi

Museo Jumex, Mexico City

Neues Museum, Berlin

ELIZABETH DILLER
Diller Scofidio + Renfro

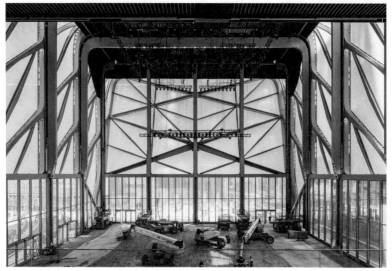

The Shed, New York City

The Broad, Los Angeles, California

XU TIANTIAN
DnA Design and Architecture

Quarry #8, Lishui, Zhejiang, China

Tofu Factory, Caizhai, Songyang, China

Frida Escobedo

2018 Serpentine Pavilion, London

Top: La Tallera Siqueiros, Cuernavaca, Mexico
Bottom: Museo Experimental el Eco, Mexico City

143

STEPHAN SCHÜTZ

gmp · von Gerkan, Marg und Partners Architects

National Museum of China, Beijing

Museum of the Culture of the Yellow River,
Zhengzhou, China

145

KERSTIN THOMPSON
Kerstin Thompson Architects

Bundanon Art Museum & The Bridge for Creative Learning, Illaroo, Australia

Monash University Museum of Art (MUMA), Melbourne, Australia

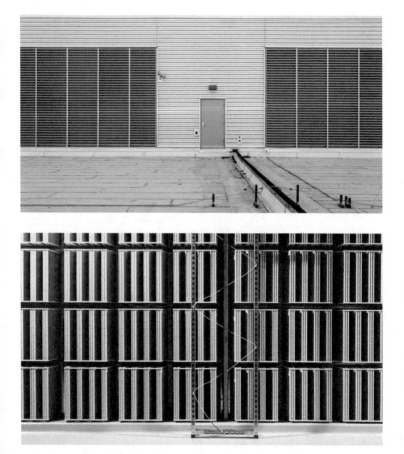

Photos of Facebook Data Center, Prineville, Oregon, featured in *Machine Landscapes: Architectures of the Post-Anthropocene,* an issue of *Architectural Design* guest-edited by Young

Stills from *New City* (2019), a series of
animated skylines of the near future
Top to Bottom:
Keeping Up Appearances
Endless Factory
Taobao Village

Lina Ghotmeh – Architecture

Interior hall view of Saradar Collection Open Storage, Mar Shaaya, Lebanon

Estonian National Museum, Tartu, Estonia

MA YANSONG
MAD Architects

Aerial rendering of Lucas Museum of Narrative Art, Los Angeles, California

Ordos Museum, Kangbashi, Inner Mongolia, China

MINSUK CHO
Mass Studies

Space K, Seoul, Republic of Korea

Model of the Danginri Podium and Promenade, part of the Power Plant, Seoul, Republic of Korea

WINY MAAS
MVRDV

Depot Boijmans Van Beuningen, Rotterdam, Netherlands

Rendering of proposed Musée Pinault (Art Mixer), Paris

KUNLÉ ADEYEMI
NLÉ

Architectural drawings of planned Lagos Art Gallery, Lagos, Nigeria

A Prelude to the Shed, a temporary structure at 10th Avenue
and 31st Street in New York City, May 2018

LI HU & HUANG WENJING
OPEN

Aerial view of UCCA Dune Art Museum, Qinhuangdao, China

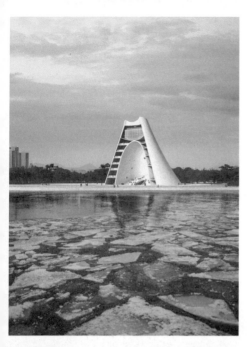

Top: Rendering of view from the sea of Sun Tower, Yantai, China
Bottom: Urban Forest, Tank Shanghai, Shanghai

ROTH – EDUARDO NEIRA
Roth Architecture

SFER IK - Tulum, Tulum, Mexico

SFER IK - Uh May, Francisco Uh May, Mexico

JING LIU & FLORIAN IDENBURG
SO – IL

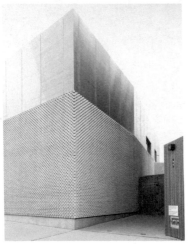

Amant Foundation, Brooklyn, New York

Centre International d'Art Verrier de Meisenthal (CIAV), Meisenthal, France

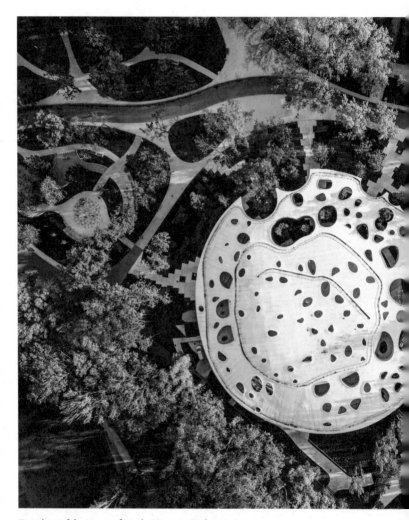

Two views of the House of Music, Hungary, Budapest

Hyde Street view of Asian Art Museum San Francisco, featuring artworks by
Chanel Miller and Jenifer K. Wofford, San Francisco, California

Grand Rapids Art Museum, Grand Rapids, Michigan

LI HU & HUANG WENJING
OPEN, Beijing

OUR SECRET WEAPON IS NATURE

I first came across the work of Li Hu and Huang Wenjing, whose Beijing-based practice is known as OPEN, when the UCCA Center for Contemporary Art, China's leading contemporary art organization, established an outpost on the northern coast of China in Bohai Bay, near the port city of Qinhuangdao. Completed in 2008, Dune, as it is called, was like nothing I had ever seen. The modest structure sits beside a wide, blue expanse of sea, barely visible. Much of the exhibition space is arrayed underground in a series of whitewashed biomorphic catacombs, burrowed under the coastal sand and covered in native grasses. The bureau's other cultural projects, such as Tank Shanghai and the futuristic Sun Tower observatory, in Yantai, likewise blend into the natural or urban environment. Fearless about questioning established institutional typologies and exuding a nascent ecological spirit, they point to a future of open possibilities for museums.

LIGHT ⟳ MUSEUM

09
22

ANDRÁS SZÁNTÓ *You established your practice in Beijing in 2008, and that's where you are based now. But you started out in the United States. Li Hu studied at Rice University and taught at Columbia. Wenjing trained at Princeton. You had both worked with influential American architects, Steven Holl and Pei Cobb Freed & Partners, respectively. Why did you name your joint practice OPEN?*

LI HU I have been thinking a lot about what it means to open a new museum in Hong Kong during a time when the world is changing so profoundly. I think change is actually a good thing. It can bring a level of energy and dynamism that is bracing but important. Change is part of the DNA.

HUANG WENJING We wished to make good design accessible to everyone.

LI HU We wanted to use architecture to convey something more meaningful, to reinvent something.

You have created remarkable art spaces: UCCA Dune Art Museum on the coast of northern China; Tank Shanghai, inside a series of converted jet-fuel tanks; and recently the Sun Tower, also by the sea. What's the common thread that runs among them?

HW One consistent thread is making public institutions accessible to everybody. Times have changed. Society has changed. And museums, too, are evolving. Tank Shanghai was a prototype for a new kind of museum. We refer to it as a museum without boundaries. It is working with the spirit of society today.

LH There are in fact several threads. One is our interest in nature. A museum can happen in between nature and our human world, sitting on the edge, at the boundary between the two. Dune and the Sun Tower both stand on the edges of urban zones, and right on the other side is nature. For the Tank, which is in a city, the plan was about inventing nature inside an urban setting. The second thread is about making each museum specific to the site—to find a unique solution to each location's problems. You need to respond to the climate, the needs, the budget, the workforce. We analyze and absorb this information, then we come up with this unique creation. And one more thread: None of our museums are conventional, by the established standards of museum typology in the Western context.

Li Hu & Huang Wenjing

The Sun Tower seems to sum up your attitudes about museums. Can you briefly describe the building?
HW I ask myself: *Is the Sun Tower even a museum?* We were not asked to design a museum. We worked with the client and proposed a new typology. It is meant to be a cultural anchor for a newly developed area, offering the missing cultural functions that a museum or a library might provide to this area. It also recognizes the power of nature. It sits directly along the shore, in one of the first locations where you can see the sun rise in China each day.

As Chinese architects of a newer generation, what experiences have shaped your understanding of museums?
LH I have worked on many museums with Steven Holl, both built and unrealized projects. I absorbed fundamental professional knowledge about what a conventional, high-quality, professional museum should be, in terms of requirements, setup, and organization. The first museum I worked on was the Nelson-Atkins Museum of Art, in Kansas City, Missouri, in 2000. Over the past twenty-two years, the world has changed tremendously, and so has the art world. In a way, now almost anything can be called a museum.
HW Working with Steven Holl and Pei Cobb Freed & Partners in New York taught us about professionalism and high-quality design. But we have never been solely interested in architecture. We are interested in large-scale innovation in the city. By luck we returned to China when the social and economic situation was changing rapidly. The society was reinventing itself. Architectural innovation was integrated with social innovation.
LH In this context, people want to reinvent the museum. But if you want to reinvent something, you first have to know what that thing is. You must master it before you break it apart. Otherwise, you just make a mess.

So in that spirit, how would you define a museum?
LH So many things today claim to be a museum. Private collectors build spaces they call museums, even if they are never open to anyone except their friends. The word *museum* is somehow being abused. For me, museums are about sharing knowledge

and about education. They need to be carefully curated, both in terms of the architecture and what is being shown. A museum must inspire dialogue through its exhibitions and public programs. However, this can take on many forms. Museum architecture must mutate or evolve together with the changing society and the changing nature of art. The concept of the art museum is totally open for reinvention.

Your practice is, perhaps to an unusual degree, focused on the future. You worked on a habitation capsule for Mars. You seem obsessed with what people in the future will need. What will that future museum need to deliver?

HW The MARS Case project, a prototype for a minimal home suitable for Mars, was designed to stimulate reflection on life on Earth today. It was about consumerism, the wastefulness in our daily lives.

LH It's not realized yet. In any case, it reflects our belief in the way humans live together, relate to each other, as a productive species.

HW We are always trying to imagine a slightly better future.

LH Not just slightly—*fundamentally* better.

But specifically, when it comes to museums, how do you imagine the experience of a visitor coming into and exploring a museum of tomorrow to be different?

HW As human beings we can never deny our biological sensitivities—our senses, our feelings. This won't change too much. Technologies will change. We will have better ways of communicating. But how we scale a space, how we perceive light, how we feel texture—those things won't change too dramatically.

LH I don't even use computers much. I am more and more returning to senses and emotions, feelings, the sort of ineffable aspects of creation. I believe in a future that is about creating experience. Museum architecture needs to foster and reinforce that experiential connection between you and what you are going to see, between what you see in one room and how it connects to the next—your connection to other people, to the city, and to the art.

Li Hu & Huang Wenjing

There are open possibilities in digital space. How do you design architecture where you have no gravity, no structural require-ments, no hard limits on cost? This open-endedness seems almost paralyzing.

LH We were recently asked to do a metaverse project, specifi-cally a virtual gallery for collectors. I have my doubts. I believe in physical connections, in the feelings of physical dimensions, and gravity as well. I also believe that art is created for specific dimensions. Even artists who create digital works still have a vision for the best way for the work to be shown. But I am curi-ous to see where this goes.

This brings us to our chosen topic, the "light institution"—a poetic term. I gather that for you this means a not-overly-defined institution, an institution of open possibilities. Can you explain what exactly you mean?

LH For us, one of the possibilities of the future is to create more democratic museums. In the past, only the super-rich could establish museums. But everybody has their own museum dreams. The light institution makes those dreams possible. It encompasses two ideas. On the one hand, you don't need to have a lot of staff to run such an institution. It might not demand a continuous influx of funding to support expensive operations. Of course, I do respect serious, established muse-ums that operate this way. But I'm talking about another way of doing things, a different future.

Second, the concept itself can be flexible: always mutating, open-minded, open-ended. We are now working on several proj-ects that incorporate digital exhibitions, as in the Sun Tower. Because the content is digital, it can be seamlessly integrated with the architecture. And because the technology can be repro-grammed, it can easily change the typology of the museum—from art to history to science to natural history to research.

The Pompidou seems to be the grandfather of this open-ended typology. Can you give me other examples that hint at this lightness?

LH The computer, or an internet browser. It can be anything. You can load it up with whatever content you want.

HW Technology is evolving fast, but architecture cannot move so quickly. You have to allow for free space and flexibility to incorporate constant changes in technology. You cannot design a building to be too specific, for certain kinds of art. Museums can now host technology summits or fashion shows. A lot of things happen in museums today that were previously inconceivable.

LH The other thing about digital exhibitions is that they can be curated remotely. You can even write the code remotely. There are tons of new possibilities to connect people and technologies.

Richard Rogers talked about "loose fit" spaces that are not too tightly defined, so they can be used for many future purposes. Was he talking about the same thing?

LH Not really. We have been discussing virtual exhibitions, but we would never be interested in working only on that type of project. In the Sun Tower, as you walk up the ramps, every time you turn you see the ocean, the changing light—you are always engaged with nature. You are not disengaged from the physical world, even when you are experiencing a digital exhibition. The two should be interlinked to create that all-important experience. Otherwise, we would just be making black boxes, like movie theaters. That would be very boring.

HW Two parallel worlds are developing: the virtual and the visceral. To us, technology, instead of canceling the real world, makes the physical more important. These two worlds must go hand in hand, especially in exhibitions.

Will a mixed-use "cultural center" that brings different cultural functions together be better suited for the future?

LH I believe that in the future the museum—and this is starting to happen—must break away from its own perimeter, out of its own box, to allow the institution to branch into other parts of social life. The museum already contains a lot more functions than just exhibitions, such as theaters and cafés. These are spaces for public life.

Should the museum building be a metaphor for what it's about, or more neutral? Should its purpose be reflected in what it looks like? I am curious what you think about this kind of metaphoric museum.

HW I see it this way: The museum has to communicate to the widest possible audience. To do so, museums cannot arrogantly say, "This is what we do; I don't care how you feel." We want museum architecture to connect to people's emotions and stimulate thoughts. In our Maritime Museum, in Shenzhen, which is shaped like a group of icebergs, we were calling attention to the climate situation, which has deteriorated to the point where even a melting iceberg at the subtropical site can be foreseeable. This striking image was designed to make people think, *Why am I seeing an iceberg in Shenzhen?*

LH Each building is like a person, with its own character, a unique nature of its own. But that character should come from a deeper source of meaning, not just from wearing something crazy as a fashion statement. Sometimes you can manifest who you are through a humble gesture. You can't put a Guggenheim Bilbao everywhere.

What we are discussing has to do with the values that inform museum buildings. What are the values, above all, you wish to see future museums embody?

LH They must be inspiring. All great architecture should touch your emotions, invigorate your senses, awaken them.
HW I agree. And, I would add, they should be engaging.
LH Welcoming, too.

By contrast, museums are often very institutional: stone, glass, hard benches—very serious.

LH Sometimes no matter how extravagant a museum building, it's still just a box with tiny doors. That is the only place to get in with your ticket. In the future, above all I hope that the museum will be more open, more inclusive, more welcoming. Of course, other things need to change fundamentally to create that sense of welcome. But the design is important to show openness and say, "Come in."

How do you translate these concerns into brick and mortar, and pixel? Architecturally speaking, what does it mean to be open and transparent?

LH You can see that in every single work of OPEN. You can enter into Dune from many places—from the top, in front, behind. This is true of the Tank as well. You can enter the front door, the back door, even jog through its campus without even realizing you have entered the space of a museum.

HW I once gave a lecture about museums as parks. Instead of imagining a museum in a park, we could think of a museum as a park. Many people who go to Tank Shanghai think they are going to a park, not a museum. Then they discover that there are exhibitions there, and they choose to step into them. This breaks down the conventional image of the museum.

Yet you are skeptical of superficial consumerism and entertainment. How do you balance people's thirst to be entertained with a seriousness of purpose?

LH I don't see these as being in conflict. There is no need to dumb down culture for the public. A good museum needs good architecture and good exhibits—good content inside. If you have great architecture and bad exhibits, it's still a failure.

Still, museum architecture can scare people away. It can suggest, "This space is not for you." This is a design dilemma.

LH Our secret weapon is nature. Look at Dune, the Tank, the Pudong Museum of Art, the Iceberg (Maritime Museum), or the Sun Tower—what draws people in, the most important attraction and tool we have, is the connection between people and nature. The tanks are surrounded by tall grasses that you might imagine to be impossible to find in an urban center. At the Sun Tower, your perception of the ocean and the sunrise is reframed as you move around it. Fundamentally, everybody loves nature. That's one thing we all have in common.

This brings me to your design process. With your emphasis on nature, how do you design a museum? Where do you start?

HW We operate in a different situation in China. Often we are designing a museum before the institution is formed, and

Li Hu & Huang Wenjing

before it has a solid collection. For better or for worse, this is the situation. We choose not to take a cynical perspective on this. Instead, we use it as an opportunity to project our vision for future museums. We know the right operator will come at a certain point. This is different from how we were working in New York, where the institution, the people, the art, were in place before you started the work.

LH In China, you must first design the brief.

HW The Iceberg was an interesting example. It was amazing we could design such a huge museum, but nobody knew what collection it would house. There was no collection.

That gives you an admirable degree of freedom. Here in the US, we are at the opposite end of the scale: Projects have too many stakeholders, tightly defined briefs, many parameters about what is and isn't possible. Some architects would envy your situation.

HW I understand what you describe precisely. For the last project I was involved in in New York, a college campus, the program brief was so thick, it was like a dictionary. There were requirements for each individual classroom. In that situation, it's hard for radical innovation to happen. You must do something safe.

You have only just gotten started, and you have done amazing things. What would be your dream project, if any museum project could be yours?

HW I have never thought about this question. We take on the projects we can get, and then we turn them into dream projects. Right now, we are working on a project called "Open Metropolis"; in Chinese it would be "city for everyone." We look at our cities and find what we miss, what we don't have but should have; then we find sites that can be improved, and we project our dream, our vision, onto them. Turning restrictions, limitations, difficulties, into a group project can be satisfying.

LH I do hope one day to build a museum in the center of a city, with a great collection, that is free for everyone. In that case, the ideal client would be the government, which doesn't need a ticket to support the museum. The dream is to design a public museum of great quality, with a great public dimension, in a city, so that everyone can easily walk right into it.

I have no doubt this will happen. Last question: Imagine you're walking through Dune or the Sun Tower as grandparents. The year is 2050. Will these buildings withstand the test of time? What will people be saying about them then?

HW A scary question. Only time can tell.

LH The same could be asked of an artist, a musician, or a writer. We all do our best to create something that could be timeless and of the highest quality, the highest level in whatever form. But how, specifically, we should do this? That I cannot answer. We try to make everything timeless.

Li Hu & Huang Wenjing

ELIZABETH DILLER
Diller Scofidio + Renfro, New York City

IT'S A CHALLENGE TO DESIGN FOR A MOVING TARGET

As a New Yorker, I can spend entire days in cultural spaces imagined or reimagined by Elizabeth Diller and her team at Diller Scofidio + Renfro. I often take a stroll along our magical public amenity, the High Line, and arrive at the Shed, the flexible interdisciplinary cultural anchor of a new neighborhood that defies conventional logic in both its physical and organizational form. I like to amble through The Museum of Modern Art, which has been rendered more welcoming and far easier to navigate by Diller's top-to-bottom renovation. I may take in a performance at Lincoln Center, which DS+R has knit into the fabric of Manhattan with a medley of sensitive design interventions. Each of these sites, along with her many others worldwide, reflects the commitments of an architect who imbibed the questioning spirit of the 1960s and who endows her projects with the restless curiosity of what she first set out to be—an artist.

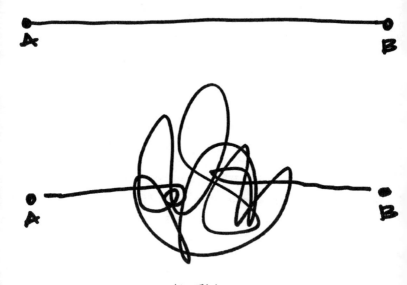

PRODUCTIVE DAY AT THE MUSEUM

ANDRÁS SZÁNTÓ *We both have eastern European roots.*
You were born in Poland and left when you were six. What are
your reflections now, seven weeks into the war in Ukraine,
when we see images daily of public buildings and even museums
being destroyed?
ELIZABETH DILLER It questions my assumptions about the
permanence of civic buildings and cities. Architects try to make
buildings more resilient to climate change, social and cultural
change, and economic fluctuations, but we never consider resilience in the face of war. When we see the vulnerability of cities
that are besieged by artillery, it's a wake-up call to the instability
of our world. As Jews, my parents survived the Holocaust in
eastern Europe. I was born in Poland, and my parents emigrated
with the family to the US in fear of another genocide. Warfare
involving civilians was unimaginable for my generation. The
ongoing coverage of civilian casualties and the geopolitical
standoff provokes a feeling of despair.

People know you as a designer of cultural buildings: the Institute
of Contemporary Art in Boston, the Shed in New York, the Broad
in Los Angeles, the expansion of The Museum of Modern Art, and
the rethinking of Lincoln Center, to name a few. You come with
a unique perspective—that of an artist and an exhibition maker,
not "just" an architect. You went to art school. How has this
shaped your outlook?
I try to see the challenge of museums from multiple points
of view: that of an architect, a curator, an artist, and an institution builder.

From the point of view of the architect, it's critically important
that the building is self-aware. Architecture is slow, geo-fixed,
and expensive. A museum of contemporary art, by definition, is
in perpetual flux. How can one possibly build for a future that's
unknowable? How can a building not get in the way of changing
artistic practices? Yet I feel the architect is responsible for
situating a building in its time, challenging conventions of the
everyday operational world and pushing the discipline. Can a
building be invisible and assertive at the same time?

From the point of view of a curator, I want the building to
allow me to tell stories that inform and challenge the public.

I need large, column-free, flexible, and technologically enabled space. From the point of view of the artist, I want space with some character that doesn't have to deal with the signature of an architect. I want grit, but also state-of-the-art infrastructure. I want height and flexibility. A white box would be quite acceptable. As a shaper of institutions, I want the building to contribute to a broader civic goal of being in dialogue with the city as well as local and global institutions. It should promote adventurous new thinking.

You talk about the agency of the artist. What about the agency of the viewer?
I believe a work is truly successful if it draws many and unexpected readings. I started to understand this when we completed the Blur Building for the 2002 Swiss Expo. Previously, we had an academic following, but the Expo put us in front of a truly diverse audience—young and old, educated and less so, natives and tourists. Despite our multiple objectives of creating weather and an architecture of atmosphere, from our critique of society's love affair with high-definition technology (Blur was decidedly low-def) and deployment of a Victorian device for creating suspense, the public came away with many other impressions that ranged from the Surrealist unconscious to the New Picturesque to religious ascension to an atomized fountain for cooling off in the summer's heat. Some children were afraid to step into it; some adults felt it was sublime. While it was initially panned by the press, which asked, "Why would anyone pay for something as undesirable as fog?" the Swiss ultimately embraced it as a symbol of the "Swiss doubt." It became wildly popular, and schoolchildren were required to visit.

This was our first mass-audience project and the point at which I began to understand that it was impossible to control the narratives of a project, as well as a sign of great success to create an interpretation machine. However, it never changed my determination to make strong architectural assertions.

You grew up in the '60s and came of age in the '70s in New York, in a particular cultural moment and situation. What imprint did that leave on you?

My education really started in the '70s, at Cooper Union. I was an art student when Hans Haacke and Hollis Frampton were teaching. Anthology Film Archives was across the street. My mind was spinning. After coming into the orbit of John Hejduk, a poet and the dean of the architecture school, I had an epiphany about space-making and transferred there. I lived in the East Village, which was gritty and dangerous and rebellious. It was impossible not to be swept up by the energy of figures like Gordon Matta-Clark, Vito Acconci, Trisha Brown, Steve Reich, Elizabeth LeCompte, and Philip Glass as they were all shattering disciplinary boundaries. Even though I was studying architecture, I never intended to be an architect—it just sort of happened.

It was a time of an intensely critical stance toward institutions and a questioning of their authority.
Yes. It was the era of the institutional critique in which museums were put into question, as were their connections to political and social structures. I was interested in alternative forms of practice and nontraditional spaces of art production and presentation. When I graduated, my partner Ricardo Scofidio and I joined forces and defined a dissident form of practice at the margins of the discipline. After gaining some exposure via self-initiated projects, we were invited by Creative Time to make several site-specific installations. Invitations to show our work then came from Artists Space and Storefront for Art & Architecture. These were all outposts of resistance to traditional museums.

Meanwhile, this was in New York, a city of great institutions— of MoMA, the Guggenheim, The Met. Were these models to follow, or icons to be toppled?
Both. In high school, I spent a lot of my time cutting school and going to MoMA to roam its collection and sketch in the Sculpture Garden. When Ric and I were invited to do an installation for the Projects Series twenty years later, we were ambivalent. On the one hand, we were delighted to be the first architects to be commissioned for the series; on the other, resistance was our knee-jerk reaction. We decided to engage the museum in a parasitic guest-host relationship.

Fast-forward to 2003, when we were invited to design our first museum, the Institute of Contemporary Art, Boston. I had a crisis of conscience. It's one thing to have a critical voice within a museum and totally another to speak in the voice of the institution as its architect. But the invitation came from a woman, a peer. I was being invited to speak in my own voice. The institutional critique no longer applied, as power was being shared. As a result of the ICA and the Broad, which followed, MoMA asked us to design their expansion in 2013. The loop had closed.

I know Cedric Price was a formative influence on you. Fun is a serious topic these days. For Price and his Fun Palace, humor was part of the equation. Are today's museums too serious?
For Cedric Price, art and entertainment were inseparable. Art was, after all, a part of life, not something sanitized for the elite. It was also unknowable. It's a challenge to design for a moving target. I take the role museums play in protecting cultural histories seriously, but for museums to stay relevant today, they have to embrace autocriticism and irony.

That's why the Fun Palace was a great reference for the Shed. It's unscripted and adaptive. The design of the Shed was driven by the things that will never change. Gravity is here to stay; thus the galleries have a huge loading capacity. There will always be a need for spaces of variable size—so the building can accommodate giant and intimate spaces. Artists will always need electrical power, which is provided in ample supply. In this "architecture of infrastructure" nothing is overdetermined.

Is there something inherently different between the creative process of an artist and that of an architect?
For me, both use a combination of the analytical and inexplicable. Both are fueled by a spirit of mischief. My process involves research, both lateral and vertical. Lateral, meaning situating myself within contemporary discourse. Vertical, meaning understanding my place in the discipline historically. I come to the table assuming someone was there before me. I want to learn before I start speaking. I often don't start with a sketch, but with writing and diagrams.

Elizabeth Diller

Either way, it all starts with a client. What makes a great client or, for that matter, a great competition?
Not everything starts with a client, actually—consider the Shed. In the first two years, we were designing a building for a theoretical institution. *The Mile-Long Opera* (2018) on the High Line was totally self-initiated. In any case, a great client is someone who has no preconceptions and trusts the process. I don't consider myself to be a problem-solver, but a problem-maker. The client has to be open to questions, not just answers. If we're working on a school, the brief may say there should be twenty-four seminar rooms and a lab. But I will ask: "What is medical education today?" Posing the bigger question allows DS+R to get past the status quo and into uncharted territory. We question everything.

The MoMA expansion, which we completed in 2019, is a good example. MoMA had a strong vision—to tell the stories of Modernism in new ways and across disciplines. We would enthusiastically eliminate media-specific galleries, but told MoMA, "Look, in addition to that, you are disconnected with the city, art is a half-mile from the front door, and the building does not give visitors any agency." MoMA was willing to work on problems they initially didn't think they had.

Most of our projects come from competitions. They are all brutal and expensive. Each time you do a competition, you fall in love with an idea, which you obsessively work out in detail. Most of the time you have your heart broken. The only thing that makes a competition great is winning.

So as a "problem-maker," how do you define a museum?
Aside from being a caretaker of cultural artifacts, a museum has the role of challenging the status quo and destabilizing norms. On the one hand, a museum should be welcoming and embracing. On the other hand, it should make visitors uncomfortable—by questioning conventions, including conventions of the museum itself. This is a paradoxical role. The museum must have gravitas and a responsibility to inform the public, but it also should slap you in the face and make you dizzy.

What can art museums learn from other types of cultural institutions, such as parks or libraries?
A lot. Like parks and recreational spaces, a visit to the museum should be a full-day affair—looking at art, having a meal, sitting in the sun, looking at art again, having a palate-cleansing break to socialize or check your email, hearing a lecture, and meeting friends for a drink. From libraries, I would adapt the idea of being quiet in public space and looking deeply into an archive, perhaps in a reading room or a space devoted to interpreting digital or print material.

This raises the question of what a successful museum visit looks like. If someone came on a lunch break to catch up on emails or take a nap, would that be a successful visit? I would say yes, because that person sees the museum as part of the fabric of life.
I totally agree. If you feel like you're just making your yearly visit, you can't feel at home, and you'll be in and out quickly. But if you treat a museum like your home, you might come often and stop by a painting that might change your life.

You are known for your urban public spaces, most famously the High Line. Museums are starting to discover connections to the city and nature. Where is the opportunity here?
Oxygen is important to museum experience. Since the Covid-19 pandemic, considering a museum without outdoor space is criminal. The Shed was somehow prescient. It was conceived as an indoor-outdoor facility. Most museums don't have outdoor space, or if they do, it's not programmed. But it's also great to have open public space to do nothing in. I think about that a lot. The High Line is full of prohibitions: You can't do sports, you can't bring your bike or Rollerblades, you can't walk your dog. You can't really do much except walk or sit. As urbanites, we're used to being productive, but the High Line rediscovered the pleasure of doing nothing but sitting or walking.

You start thinking of Walter Benjamin and his figure of the flâneur.
Exactly. You are walking with no aim but to wander.

Elizabeth Diller

*So how can architects build museum now that will be indis-
pensable in, let's say, fifty years?*
To be indispensable, the museum cannot be seen as a luxury,
but rather as a common necessity. It should welcome all audiences. It could be decentralized, with satellites across the entire
city. It would not be a silo, but a piece of cultural infrastructure
that's connected to education and to nonvisual artforms—and
to city hall, because it would want to have some influence on
policy. And it might have a great bar, and be a place where you
can eat, drink, and hang out twenty-four hours a day. It would
be connected to other parts of the globe, a cultural hub linked
to other hubs internationally, to create a discourse not limited
by geography. Maybe the museum should not be a thing, but
a system.

*A seductive vision, for sure. But many people still find museums
elitist and exclusionary, partly because of their buildings.*
Most museums isolate themselves from the "abject" street. If
you can walk into a museum off the street, on the same surface
that you walk on as a citizen, that's a gesture toward connecting
to everyday life. Contemporary architecture has a bad rap. Audiences feel alienated by it. Artists are typically allergic to it. It's
important to prove them wrong and design museums that make
artists and audiences feel uninhibited.

*You already talked about the museum as an agent of good gover-
nance. Much discussion around museums today concerns equity
in terms of income, race, gender. How can architecture help
nurture that equity?*
It seems we did something right at the Broad, in Los Angeles.
It has the most diverse visitor demography of any museum in
the US, with 64 percent of its visitors identifying as non-white. It
also has the youngest visitors, with an average age of thirty-two,
compared to the national average of forty-six. Why is that?
Partly it's the luxury of free admission. But there is something
else. We decided to not have an admission desk, nor an information desk. You just come in off the street into a lobby and
go straight into the galleries. No one tells you where to go. It's
intuitive, with almost no signage. There are no guards, only a

docent team of art students and artists. I think this is part of the Broad's success. There is an absence of institutional authority.

Perhaps architecture is not necessarily what turns people away. It may be the institutional attitude.
Agreed, but they're connected. Museum entrances are usually transactional spaces. You come in, you pay, you get your ticket, leave your coat, get a stub, and get directions. I find it a turnoff. When you leave the city street, how many thresholds do you have to pass through to get to the art? When you get in front of the art, you feel that eyes are on you to make sure you're not too close. Why not put art as close to the street as possible, if not on the street itself, and rely more on electronic ticketing and smart coat-check services? The museum façade can be the first canvas.

We started out by talking about institutional critique. Today, we are once again in a moment when many are throwing grenades at the museum. What advice would you have for a young architect still in grenade-lobbing mode?
It's important to go through this phase in your life. Be outraged. Express your resistance. There is a lot to be angry about. But ultimately, as I tell my students, get a seat at the table—engage the powers that be. That's the lesson I learned personally: When you're working from the periphery, it's hard to mobilize change. Instead of working from the margins, you can walk through the front door and change the system stealthily.

Also, we have to reconcile ourselves to the fact that institutions require expertise, leadership, and money. It's part of the deal. And that's okay. You sometimes have to navigate bureaucratic complexity to get a result you're passionate about. Having a critique is not enough. You need a generative vision.

Elizabeth Diller

BJARKE INGELS
BIG | Bjarke Ingels Group, Copenhagen, New York City,
London, Barcelona, Shenzhen

A MUSEUM COULD
BE A WAKE-UP CALL

Time is what first introduced me to the boyish, restless,
iconoclastic Bjarke Ingels—or more precisely, horology did. Audemars Piguet, the venerable Swiss watchmaking manufacture based in a remote valley in the
Jura Mountains, had decided to erect a Musée Atelier
Audemars Piguet to showcase its craft and heritage.
I advocated for the then-up-and-coming Danish architect and took part in some early planning. Nothing
could have prepared me for the outcome, nor did it
resemble any museum I had seen before: a translucent
swirl of glass evoking the spring coil of a timepiece
sitting elegantly in the landscape, illuminated from
within—itself an embodiment of the marvels of preci-
sion engineering. Ingels likes to tell stories with
buildings. The museum in his hands becomes an
exhibition. Yet his larger passion points to a more
urgent shared predicament. He is working to deploy
architecture to save the planet. And he believes
museums can join the effort.

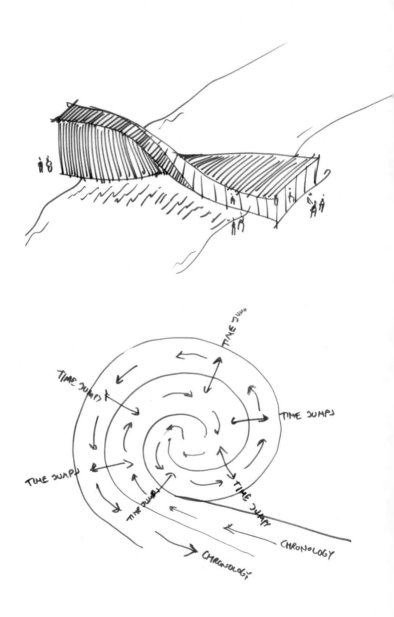

TIME JUMPS

TIME JUMPS

TIME JUMPS

TIME JUMPS

TIME JUMPS

TIME JUMPS

TIME JUMPS

CHRONOLOGY

CHRONOLOGY

ANDRÁS SZÁNTÓ *You're Danish. Architecture and design are in your blood, from modern furniture to the Louisiana Museum of Modern Art outside Copenhagen. This must be a blessing, but also a curse. After all, much of the world doesn't conform to this level of design purity.*

BJARKE INGELS You remind me of a visit to the Louisiana, which is the most perfect fusion of architecture, art, and nature you can imagine. In Denmark, everything is beautifully designed, and the society also functions well. While we were there, a four-year-old came over, took my hand, and asked me to help him find his parents—a subtle testament to this idyllic, almost too perfect society.

The Danish word for design is *formgivning*. To design is to give form to something that has not yet been given form; in other words, to design a fragment of the future. Denmark is the most egalitarian country in the world. There is extreme conformity. How can radical experimentation emerge from such a primordial soup of consensus? Because we are constantly forced to make everybody happy. We turn the culture of consensus into a radical agenda to make everyone happy.

I finally made it to the Musée Atelier Audemars Piguet, the horology museum you designed in Le Brassus. I remember when it was a drawing: a giant coil sitting in the hayfields. Did it turn out as you imagined?

One hundred percent. Partly because in Switzerland, vocational training has not lost its value. In the US and parts of Europe, making something with your hands has been deemed inferior to academic pursuits. In Switzerland, it requires years of serious education to become a metalworker or mason or carpenter.

I'm sure you met with the watchmakers who put ornamentation on parts of the watch you will never see—because God can see it.

If there is someone who has a fundamental appreciation for quality of execution in the finest detail, that, of course, is a watchmaker. The architecture we came up with—an "open-worked" structure where the building reveals everything—is similar to the watch I am wearing. It's the magic of all the things working together. The metal roof is made of steel and brass, to keep it light. The curved glass walls are not only room dividers that solve acoustics and separation, but also the load-bearing structure that carries the floating roof. Every architectural element contributes to this holistic ensemble, like the gears coming together in a clock.

You've designed striking museums, including the Maritime Museum of Denmark, on the sea, and the Twist Museum, shaped like a bridge, in Norway. Each is different, but what is your overall perspective on museums that has shaped these projects?
Working on the Musée Atelier Audemars Piguet, we discovered this relationship between form and content—or the hardware and software. In watchmaking, as in architecture, the form is the content. The choice of materials and how they are shaped and manipulated are what delivers the function—just as in architecture, where the choice of materials, the sequence of spaces, and the way you let in the light somehow creates the experience. Of course, you can have a digital watch that just tells the time, as you can have a building that is just a raw accumulation of space. But then you won't get this wonderful synergy that is found in classic watchmaking and architecture.

Some of the museums we have created are for art, like the Twist and La MÉCA, in Bordeaux. But many are for other things, like the Maritime Museum of shipping. For the museums with a more specific focus, you can pursue a more intimate relationship between the building and its content. Art exhibitions require more freedom and flexibility to accommodate radically different expressions. One must gauge how much character a space should have, so that there is something for the art to dialogue with, but without overpowering the artistic expression that lives within this environment.

Your projects are often driven by a big idea that also expresses the purpose of the building. The Musée Atelier Audemars Piguet references a spring coil. The Maritime Museum integrates a dry dock. LEGO House is modular. The Twist, an art museum, is basically a sculpture. These buildings are symbols, exhibits. Why blend museum and exhibit this way?
As an architect, you must capture not only the likeness of the

institution or the program, but also the personality, the future potential, the soul of this subject. The Twist—a *kunsthalle* more than an art museum—is situated in a sculpture park called Kistefos that was already quite established. They had organized summer exhibitions in a barn, and they wanted to take it up a notch. We came up with the idea that we could get the most space for the museum if we suspended it over the river that runs through the park. The building becomes part of the journey, so as you walk through the sculpture park, the museum takes you from one side to the other. The building turns from horizontal to vertical in a kind of twist, creating a striking sculptural form—a sculpture in a sculpture park, but also a bridge across a river, and an art museum.

Museums have long revealed their intentions. Museums that were built to look like Greek temples were thematic that way. They said, "This is a place of high culture." But those messages can become out of date. How do you future-proof expressive architecture?
That comes down to the core of this conversation—the relationship between form and content, or hardware and software, the exhibition space and the exhibit itself. You could say that in a lot of the expressive architecture that came in the wake of the Guggenheim in Bilbao, the expression was dissociated from the content. It was almost at odds with it. Frank Lloyd Wright's Guggenheim was maybe the first of its kind, with its strong and exhibition-driven logic of the descending spiral. It is celebrated and detested as an exhibition space, because it does create certain demands. The way we work is an extension of that way of looking at architecture. You establish certain logics that revolve around the performance of the building as an exhibition, and then you pursue that experiment to its fullest extent.

Where else do you see this merger of the museum and the exhibition?
Look at the LEGO museum. LEGO is, of course, a building and playing system. It is a world-creation tool. We similarly wanted to be inviting, engaging, and playful. You can enter from all four corners. Inside, the light seeps in between the galleries that hover above you. You can climb on the roofs, which are interconnected playgrounds. It is one of few museums where you are

invited to touch. The architecture is blocky, bricky, and tectonic, with loosely interconnected elements. At street level, it is pretty subtle, with white-glazed ceramic tiles in the same modularity as LEGO bricks. Everything is paved with the colorful rubber often found in playgrounds. So on the one hand, it is subtle and museal, and on the other hand, colorful and playful—catering to this idea of taking "play" seriously.

It's also entertaining. Today people want some level of experience and spectacle. How do you balance seriousness with this contemporary desire for entertainment?
It is important to distinguish between entertainment and engagement. Entertainment has an element of passive consumption, and the world is full of that. Engagement, by contrast, is about encouraging the visitor to take active part in the exploration of the environment. The smartest minds and the most valuable companies in the world are waging a war for our attention. If we can create an environment that engages us, and that makes us fully present, that is a gift that we can give as architects to the people who spend time in our buildings.

That is perhaps the essence of what we can do in museums. A museum could be a wake-up call that pulls you out of all those distractions and into the present. That is similar to the power of art. The art that I love expands my perception of the world. Once you have opened your eyes and ears to this expanded appreciation of the world, you can no longer look at it in the same way. The architectural environment can help you have that experience—to be fully present and fully engaged.

So the role of the architect and the museum is to make this magic happen?
Can you show great art in a shitty building? Yes, you can. A studio visit is always exciting, to see where the work is made. My own offices are almost all in former warehouses because of the generosity of the space, the free daylight, and the long spans for creative freedom. This somewhat industrial aesthetic is what you find in a lot of artists' studios and in many museums. For MÉCA in Bordeaux, we put a theater, library, and art museum in a building made of prefabricated concrete, creating a space almost

Corbusian in its rawness. The exhibition space is essentially a steel roof with skylights and concrete floors. The '70s era was obsessed with flexibility in the extreme. So you ended up with exhibition spaces that were so generic that they had no character or materiality at all, just white drywall. That is clearly not the greatest way to challenge the artist or the visitor.

I like to say that the white cube is a period room. It's an anachronism, in a way.
That's a great distinction. Yes, it is a period room. It has a certain sensibility. It is too bad he is no longer alive, because Hans Hollein would have been great to interview for your book. He created some of the best art museums, in Frankfurt and Mönchengladbach, which are, in their own wild ways, masterpieces. We like to engage the visitor by contradicting expectations. I often say the autopilot is a terrible designer. There should be a reason why a building is the way it is. When it is designed by autopilot, we end up with generic spaces and missed opportunities. And we lull the visitor to sleep.

Your firm's credo is that "architecture is the art and science of making sure our cities and buildings fit with the way we want to live our lives." Can you make a building that makes sense fifty years from now?
Of course. Consider the Louisiana Museum. What gives it a sense of timelessness is that constant exploration of the relationship between inside and outside, with the garden—the largest gallery in the museum—at the center. The museum is executed in a limited palette of white Scandinavian Modernism. The galleries are a journey through seventy years of Danish architecture. This brings us back to your statement about the white cube being a period room. The timelessness of Louisiana is that it has remained faithful to an archetypical relationship— the one between inside and outside—and kept true to the period when it originated.

So how, ultimately, will tomorrow's museums look and feel different? What will surprise us about them?
With the arrival of crypto and NFTs, the art world has achieved a

certain confidence in digital art. Museums are going to have to grapple with the idea of virtual art and how to experience it. Everybody in the technology and the design sectors is trying to imagine-predict-invent what the metaverse means. For museums and exhibitions, it is going to be a great field of exploration.

For now these digital spaces feel rather disappointing. For starters, they are too real. They have floors; they appear to have gravity. Virtual museum spaces will require a new design language. We worked with a firm called Within, led by Chris Milk and Aaron Koblin, to fantasize about a virtual museum of art. We believe you have to navigate it intuitively as a human being. We took advantage of the fact that the rules of gravity don't apply in virtual space, so we designed a Möbius strip as a continuous street of galleries. As you're walking, you can look up, and the horizon above you is gently warping and distorting, and when you have walked the loop, you will have walked on both sides. We will need to experiment to ensure that what you're experiencing feels somehow real and relevant. There may be a co-evolution between technology and visitor expectations. Take too great a leap, and you might simply lose the audience.

You and your colleagues are heavily invested in advances in engineering. You're working on a Mars project, and on 3D printing. Museums have sometimes served as test cases for daring engineering solutions—from the Guggenheim to Centre Pompidou to Calatrava's museums. Are they experimental enough?
The Centre Pompidou is the manifestation of something I have previously criticized: this excitement about overflexibility. They avoided being generic by celebrating the colorful cacophony of 1970s building systems. There is a neoconservatism in current museum architecture, which may be a counterreaction to a post-Bilbao overexcitement about random expressiveness for the sake of attention. This may be an overcorrection.

For NASA, we are working with ICON, a 3D-printing company that develops advanced construction technologies. We are trying to apply the promise of additive manufacturing and automation to the built environment. And 3D printing may make

Bjarke Ingels

elaborate design a commodity. Complex geometries, warping, architectural refinement, detail, and form may come at almost no cost. This could lead us to a new Art Nouveau, Jugendstil, or Art Deco revival, opening up new possibilities. We may find ourselves back in a pre–Adolf Loos world. Ornament will be free, more democratic—a kind of re-enchantment of architecture.

Maybe architecture will be more ornamental again. Maybe it will be about really thoughtfully sculpted transitions from one environment to another. When every machine has the skill set of the world's best Japanese cabinetmaker, there will be no limit to what you can imagine and afford. To neglect tectonic creative abundance would be a monumental missed opportunity. We won't necessarily end up in a new Baroque. But failing to embrace this technology would be like closing your eyes to where the world is going.

We may, ironically, find ourselves in exuberantly decorated museums that house dematerialized digital art. "Step inside this neo-Baroque museum for a virtual experience." Let us switch to ecology, an area where you have ventured deeply. Where is the museum in this urgent moment of reckoning about ecology?
I think the role of any building type, including the museum, is to use it as an experiment that can be celebrated and scaled. We have opened the world's most environmentally friendly furniture factory, entirely powered by hydroelectricity, in the Norwegian forest. We are building the largest urban-integrated photovoltaic installation in the heart of Milan. We are making a research center for the New European Bauhaus in Seville, in a building that produces twice as much energy as it consumes. We just won the new Zürich airport, which will be entirely mass timber to capture the identity of Switzerland, with the whole roof comprised of photovoltaic cladding. At the Google Bay View headquarters, the entire roof is a photovoltaic "dragonscale." In all these cases, sustainable solutions become an essential part of the architecture and the experience within. Museums, as public buildings, can call attention to the necessity of this engagement with sustainability, so the visitors will be pulled into the present not just by the art, but by a building that performs differently.

Can architecture address our largest, systemic problems?
The answer is a big, roaring yes. But it does require a courage and confidence to address things at scale. Right now, there is a kind of insecurity in the profession. We rarely dare to address big issues anymore. But if design is giving form to the future, then each time we as architects are called upon to design a corner of that future—and if that corner is a museum—then we can make that little corner of the world a utopian manifestation of what we know the future could be.

That means making the museum inclusive and engaging to a larger audience. It means locating museums strategically to elevate their neighborhoods. In Buenos Aires, they are putting public buildings into the favelas. Rather than moving that population into new neighborhoods, they are moving the city into those neighborhoods, so they are elevated with public investment. Museums can do the same. We can make sure that museums are pioneers, part of the avant-garde—not just the artistic avant-garde, but the social avant-garde.

You were born in 1974, but it seems you are just getting started. What alliances will you need to build to achieve the impact you want, and can museums be part of them?
We are working with a major Danish shipping company to reimagine ten of their large container terminals around the world as green growth hubs. By having a huge demand, they can convert the entire port ecosystem, the entire city, and potentially the country to renewables. Those ports can accelerate the green energy transition. Those are the kind of alliances we would not previously have had as architects.

Museums also have a remarkable opportunity to awaken public interest and awareness. They can have a huge impact as experiments to put a small, pragmatically realized piece of utopia into action. The impact of such a museum would vastly exceed its scale as a building. That's where I see the true power of museums in terms of world impact.

A museum in every green port. That would be a utopia. Let's build it.
Exactly.

MA YANSONG
MAD Architects, Beijing, Jiaxing, Los Angeles, Rome

MUSEUMS ARE THE STARTING POINT OF A JOURNEY

In *The Future of the Museum: 28 Dialogues*, the precursor to this volume, Sandra Jackson-Dumont, director of the Lucas Museum of Narrative Art, currently under construction in Los Angeles, described the intentions of the new institution this way: "Through visual storytelling, we will expand the role of art and of museums in society." The task of translating this vision into a physical building fell to Ma Yansong, among the most prolific members of a younger generation of Chinese architects and founder of the Beijing-based MAD Architects. MAD has designed strikingly expressive cultural facilities across China and the world. And the Lucas Museum, like the cinematic work of its namesake, is nothing if not futuristic. It embodies the forty-seven-year-old architect's belief in *surreality*—the idea that a museum building should transport visitors outside of this world, allowing them to escape everyday worries and routines.

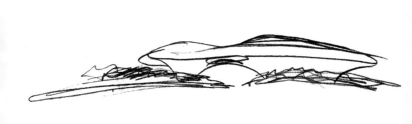

ANDRÁS SZÁNTÓ *You are a prolific maker of museums. What is the opportunity for a museum architect in China today?*
MA YANSONG I don't think there is such a thing as a *museum architect*, especially in China. They are the same architects who were building cities, houses, towers, commercial buildings. As the market changes, most cities have built too many commercial buildings, and now they need cultural centers. This generates many opportunities, including for architects who are already successful.

MAD Architects was founded in 2004. In the early days we didn't have many projects that could be realized, so we didn't build many commercial projects either. We are the architects for people who are looking for something special. Most cities just want a cultural building—because they must have one—and they just need to finish the job. But some of them are looking for something more. They want to think about the purpose of a cultural building. They have deeper questions about the identity and future of their city. We can give them answers.

You have talked about how architecture can give urban centers a soul. When you were forty, you published a manifesto, Shanshui City, *arguing that architecture should serve people and nature, not capital and power. Where does the museum fit into this picture?*
I grew up in Beijing. Old Beijing is a beautiful city built hundreds of years ago with many features, such as hills and lakes of different scales. For the modern mindset these elements are just simply beautiful. I think they are, in fact, the very soul of the city. And that is exactly what's missing from our modern cities, where everything has to be "useful" and has to have practical value. If everything is useful, then people will have nowhere to escape. They cannot find spiritual freedom. It is the task of a cultural space to provide that freedom. In the short term, museums should be spaces where people can escape from reality. In the long term, museums should help people build their own spiritual worlds, their own individual worlds, where they are free to imagine.

You studied at Yale University, and you worked for Zaha Hadid. Who or what are your touchstones when it comes to architecture?
Beijing. My childhood, my memories of old Beijing, are the most important influences. I only spent two years at Yale, and only one semester with Zaha, and then I worked with her in London for one year. She brought me into the contemporary art scene. Being an architect means trying to challenge everything around you—and that is who she was, always pushing boundaries. But I don't like it when an architecture studio turns into a big corporate firm with a specific identification, like Zaha or Frank Gehry. MAD is still young, and we don't want to look like a brand. If there is something consistent in my work, it is that I want to find something different in each project.

You also make art. Ink Ice, *for example, was a 2006 installation of ink in ice that melted over three days. You collaborated with Olafur Eliasson. How does making art inform your thinking about architecture?*
It's just a way of thinking. I can do architecture. I can make movies. I could produce music if I knew the techniques. Architecture is just one language among many. Art and architecture talk about the same issues. But I don't want to bring art into architecture. Architecture is powerful on its own. It has functions and technical features. Above all, it is a space for people—and people are emotional. Emotion is the ultimate destination for all architecture.

Some museums seem to be in the service of art; others seem to compete with it. Hadid made some buildings in which, to be honest, it is hard for the art to breathe. What's your view?
Architecture absolutely should work with the content. Even if the content only needs a simple space, it doesn't mean that it can't be special. If the content is about inspiring people, then the building cannot be boring. The building should and must follow the purpose of art, which is to inspire. Architecture has its own language to help people prepare for that journey. It should talk to the art, to the content, but also to the city and history around the museum.

Ma Yansong

How do you define a museum?
A museum is a place for people to escape from reality and dive into another surreal world.

What are some of the things that get in the way of diving in like that?
Sometimes a museum makes you focus too much on the content. When I study, I don't want to only read, read, read—I want a moment to relax and think. Some museums are too full, there's just too much. I like museums where you can enjoy the art and, at the same time, you can enjoy the presence of other people and the environment around you.

There is research to show that when you display a lot of art in a space, it makes people tired. Seeing a lot of art on a wall stim- ulates peripheral vision, which is linked to our perception of external threats and uses up a lot of brain energy. But let's talk about the wider world around the museum. Society is changing. The world is changing. How must architecture adapt?
I think architecture has sacrificed too much for green technol- ogy. Just because you have a better air conditioner or thermal glass doesn't mean it is better architecture. Sometimes I see new buildings that are "sustainable" or "green," but the spatial quality is the same as in the last century—same heights, same configurations. Focusing too much on technology makes archi- tecture a product, which at its core is commercial; it changes every year, and it will soon be outdated. Not that I'm saying green technology isn't important. Traditional gardens and temples used natural materials, of course, but it was all about the experience and how people feel the materials.

The challenge is to build museums that will make sense fifty or a hundred years from now, when the way people live will be very different. How do you anticipate that?
I believe that when a building is personal, it can last a long time. It becomes a medium for people to communicate across generations. We want to visit those buildings because they are so inspiring, so artistic, so crazy. We want to feel what architects created in their minds, like Antoni Gaudí. A museum building

should do that with a similar sense of authorship, as proof that our civilization is formed by inspiring minds.

People in the museum field have expressed a need for a more community-minded, transparent, socially engaged museum. This is the new software of the museum. How can architecture respond or lead the way?
I absolutely agree. But that doesn't mean museum architecture should be commonplace. It should still have a strong identity. When people come to a museum, they should feel things. A space can engage people with an attitude of openness. You can make it open, welcoming, engaging, and interactive. From my experience, you have to make the architecture interesting, so people don't come only for the content, but also because they think, *This space is inviting me*. I hate the idea of art being exclusive. It makes museums so closed.

You grew up in a time of massive urbanization in China. Can a museum help the city achieve a better version of itself?
Sure, especially in China. Most cultural institutions in China were founded by governments. They were placed strategically at key locations. And if we think of a museum as a means of activating the city, then the museum should be able to take on multiple forms, not just grand buildings. Rem Koolhaas did a museum with a private developer—the Times Museum, in Guangzhou—where they put the museum on the top floor of a residential tower. That is an interesting idea: to embed the museum into urban life.

The museum was born in Europe and raised in America. It is a Western construct. What will be the impact of this great wave of Chinese museum construction?
In China the hardware usually comes first. Many places are determined to build opera houses and music halls, but many of them do not have enough content to fill the space. When designing these buildings, you don't even necessarily know what kind of collections they'll display—history, natural history, art? Now, more and more young people from the younger generations who have art or history backgrounds are passionate about influencing how museums operate.

Ma Yansong

Have you been asked to design any digital spaces? What would museum design look like if it could free itself from the usual constraints of architecture, like gravity and budgets? Have you had to think about this?

We have been invited to create several projects in the digital sphere. What interests me about the metaverse is that it can enable you to fully escape reality—it can be all about imagination. But I don't want to become a fantasy creator. I want to create a world in the metaverse that people can believe and experience. They should believe that such a space could, in fact, be a reality. This could be a way to convince people to trust that they can do something more ambitious in reality. Then I can more easily bring my architectural ideas into that reality. The true experience of museums can only be felt inside the physical place. What the metaverse can do better is create community, which is another purpose of the museum.

You already said that a museum should transport you beyond everyday life—the idea of surreality—so let's explore this a little deeper. Tell me more about the museum as a place to escape reality.

I think museums are the starting point of a journey. You don't want everyone to come out of the museum feeling the same. I believe that everyone should start their journey from the same place, but that each journey should be different.

And where does this journey lead?

People only spend a few hours in the museum each time, similar to going to a movie theater or reading a book. What's amazing is that when you finish a movie or close a book, you can find your emotional or spiritual world. It should be the same with museums.

Is that a kind of escape, a break from uniform, everyday life?

Yes. That is the first step. When a movie starts and people step away temporarily from their real lives, they are ready for the journey. The same is true for a journey in a museum.

This seems more like the kind of transformation people might seek in a place of worship, in a spiritual place—it is an architecture of transfiguration, one that pulls you out of and away from your life.
I agree. The museum is a church for art, a space for imagination and free thinking. That is the purpose of the museum. It is not just a showcase.

It does seem that Surrealism, in the artistic sense, is having a moment. The title of the 2022 Venice Biennale exhibition, The Milk of Dreams, *came from a Surrealist work by Leonora Carrington. Major museums like The Met have recently mounted big Surrealism exhibitions. Why do you think it is suddenly everywhere?*
I mean, the world itself is surreal. More important, I think surreality can help everyone appreciate the value of imagination. It can inspire people and can set them free, or make them feel that they can be free themselves, so that they can imagine or try something for themselves.

Speaking of the imagination, I got to know your work when I was interviewing the director of the Lucas Museum of Narrative Art in Los Angeles, which some would say is a surreal city.
George Lucas is an artist who tells great stories. The world loves his movies. He creates a new world, a spiritual world. I think a museum tries to do the same, to inspire more people. That is why the museum has a lot of educational functions. At the Lucas Museum, they will work with artists, creatives, local schools, and young people in the neighborhood, among others. The architecture should make people feel curious and excited, especially young people.

A critic asked me, "Why don't you make this museum the same as other USC [University of Southern California] buildings, with red brick, so they harmonize with one another?" I said the way a building talks with a city is one thing, but to talk to people is another. The architectural form and the materials of the Lucas Museum of Narrative Art are very innovative. That will make young people want to come and stay there and engage. They can open their minds and talk and think—the architecture helps them do that. The original concept of this building was

Ma Yansong

a floating canopy, because the first time I visited the site I saw a big tree. It was beautiful. That was my inspiration. I imagined students going to class in surrounding schools and sitting under this tree canopy for extracurricular knowledge after school.

Is there perhaps a contradiction here? On the one hand, museum buildings should transport you, like a fantasy. On the other hand, they should blend in and be part of life. How do you make it surreal, but not too surreal?
All my buildings do that. Each place is unique. When I am building something in the center of Beijing or in a historical city like Rome, I choose to be more low-key. Sometimes in China, the area around a building doesn't have anything particularly special. In that way, it needs strong, powerful architecture to set the mood or be the soul of the neighborhood.

Can you tell me more about your work process, your way of designing? How do you proceed to that idea, whether it is a pow-erful one or a more restrained one?
The visit to the place is important. Each location has a mood—the weather, the season. Sometimes I have a strong feeling on the first visit. Once you have those feelings, you just need to sketch it out. There have been a few times that I didn't feel anything. Then I would try to gather more information and do more site visiting. The first instinct is usually powerful.

I understand that in China often the client doesn't have a strong view about the building program. But you have also worked a lot internationally. What is a great client for you?
We avoid clients who don't respect designers—who give too many comments. I usually have a strong idea about what we want to do, but we need a partner to discuss how to make it all work. A good client can be really valuable. They understand your vision and they are on the same track, and they care about the details. I want this kind of partnership.

What about competitions?
As a young firm, we started out by doing competitions. We won some and got the chance for people to see our works. But in

general I think every architect hates competitions. Unless your projects or clients don't need your creativity, in which case a competition can be a way to express your idealism.

Nature is central to your work. How should it relate to museum architecture?
I am interested in the beauty of nature and how people communicate with nature. The quality of this communication should be on a spiritual or emotional level. All architecture should prioritize spiritual quality—the functions and technological advancements are secondary. Why do the Japanese put sand in their gardens? What is its function? It is a metaphor. It influences how you feel. We need nature to keep our relationship with the existing world and to help us imagine a bigger world, or a better future.

I am thinking about the Louisiana Museum of Modern Art, in Denmark. That museum is a beautiful journey. The scale of the building makes me think more of myself. I can see the beautiful landscape. I can see other people and the art that is correlated to it. I don't know if such a museum could ever have the same number of visitors as The Met in New York, but maybe the deeper connection between people and nature is more important.

I would like to close with a reflection on your generation. You are still young by the standards of your profession—born in 1975— but old enough to have memories of growing up in the traditional hutongs *of Beijing. What, in the end, is the responsibility of your generation of Chinese architects?*
To shape a space where people can find a mindset of freedom, where they can feel inspired to imagine. For China, with such a long history and such a large population, prioritizing diversity and individual imagination is the most important thing. The museums we build for sure should present knowledge. But museums should also be able to inspire people to feel and explore the minds of artists, who create all the beauty of our world.

Ma Yansong

SOU FUJIMOTO
Sou Fujimoto Architects, Tokyo

AN OPEN FIELD OF ACCEPTANCE

Imagine a circular building in a park. Trees give way
to a clearing as you approach the jewel-like pavilion.
Some trees stand right next to the structure's glass
curtain wall; others pierce through irregularly shaped
holes in an undulating canopy high overhead, offering up glimpses of open sky. There is hardly a boundary separating building and green space. This is Sou
Fujimoto's House of Music, Hungary, a hybrid exhibition and performance space that opened in 2021 in
Budapest's City Park, on the former grounds of the
1896 Millennial Exhibition. The underside of the building's canopy is decorated with a golden latticework of
leaves—a nod to the Academy of Music, a beloved Art
Nouveau concert hall. The House of Music is an example of the Hokkaido-born Fujimoto's commitment to
contextually sensitive architecture that is embedded
in its cultural environment and, above all, pays homage
to nature.

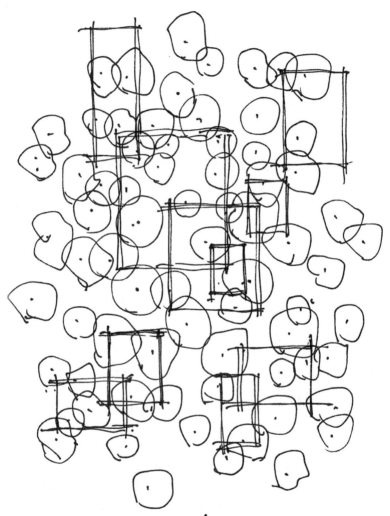

museum as FOREST / FOREST as MUSEUM.

ANDRÁS SZÁNTÓ *I know you are interested in the future. In 2018 you even organized an exhibition of your work titled* Futures of the Future. *How do you see your architecture fitting into that future?*

SOU FUJIMOTO Whenever I think about a new project, I always like to make something a little bit new, to open a small door to the future. At the same time, for almost twenty years I have been talking about a "primitive future." Design for the future has to be based on fundamentals: the body, human communications, the cave, or a nest of animals. For me, the future is not "futuristic" at all. It is linked to primary and fundamental phenomena. In this respect nature is key, because we humans have been living with nature all along. We need to think of the architecture of the future always in relation to nature.

It's impossible for me not to mention your link to Budapest, the city where I was born. In 2021 you completed the House of Music there, a kind of museum of music. It is an example of what we're going to talk about later—a museum with green space around it and even inside it. Are you pleased with how it turned out?

Of course, yes. Budapest's City Park is full of nature, but it is an artificial park—nature maintained by people. The relationship between people and nature was established long ago. Of course, the link to the history of music in Budapest was already important. The golden leaves under the canopy of the House of Music were inspired by the Art Nouveau Academy of Music. When I won the competition, they took me there. I was impressed by the classical ceiling covered with all these golden leaves. I like this link to history and nature.

Making a big building in a man-made park was a challenge. We decided to make transparencies and floating roofs, and a large exhibition space underground, so the architecture almost melts into the greenery. In the autumn, when the leaves turn gold or red, I expect the building will almost seem to vanish. Under the canopy the interior and exterior spaces become continuous and connected to the park. Finally, harmony was important. Architecture should always be in beautiful harmony with its surroundings.

You grew up in Hokkaido, in a rural area, so you had ample exposure to nature before moving to big cities. How did that color your outlook?

It was essential. When I was a kid I didn't much notice the nature around me; I just played in the forest and the fields. I re-recognized the richness of my hometown after moving to Tokyo. Yet even dense, busy Tokyo, with its narrow alleys, seems to me fundamentally similar to my hometown. It's made up of small-scale crowded situations, so many random layers. The structure of the forest is similar. Tokyo is like an artificial forest. I don't like to divide nature and artifacts completely. I like to find a point where they melt together.

You opened your Tokyo practice in 2000. In Japan you are surrounded by this incredible legacy of beautiful museum design, part of a national tradition of design minimalism and perfect-ionism. It is wonderful, but perhaps also a little constraining. How did that influence you?

It was a challenge to think about this tradition. In traditional Japanese architecture there are almost no boundaries between architecture and gardens. They interact via open, in-between spaces. Of course, I had experienced Tadao Ando's museums, which often include indoor spaces that are open to the out-doors—these in-between situations. I saw many re-translations of the Japanese tradition of minimalism into contemporary architecture. The question became: What should I do?

I don't like a strategy that is too straightforward. I like to find hidden, primary forces behind the superficial appearances of traditions. I read about Tōru Takemitsu, the Japanese composer who tried to find a middle ground between Western and Eastern music, or between the sounds of nature and composed music. He was a great inspiration. Finally, I made a private house, House N, a box-in-a-box composition where we tried to create in-between spaces and bring nature inside. We all struggle to find our own reinterpretations of Japanese traditions. They are a great starting point for us.

A seeming absence of boundaries is a hallmark of your structures. They are light on the ground. You can see right through them,

*like your 2013 Serpentine Pavilion. It is beautiful, but it speaks
an architectural language quite far from that of most museums—
because museums have boundaries and enclosures, or traditionally they do.*

That is a good contradiction. When we see a contradiction, we
can be creative and go beyond it. Even if we had a museum in
the middle of nature, we would need a box to store delicate
art pieces in it. We always seek to establish a good interaction
between outside and inside. How do you do that? Glass is an
easy solution. The Serpentine Pavilion was an extreme case, an
experiment to redefine the fixed boundaries of architecture—no
strong columns, no strong walls, nor strong roofs or window
openings, but still a sense of enclosure. As a conceptual trial it
was a success. On the other hand, I realized that if you like to
make architecture, you do need stronger boundaries.

*I imagine some museums you have seen on your travels must
have influenced you. What are your icons—the achievements we
cannot ignore?*

I was deeply influenced by the Neue Nationalgalerie in
Berlin, by Mies van der Rohe, recently refurbished by David
Chipperfield: this extreme space, something beyond the definition of an art space or art museum in its time. On the other
hand, I love the Kimbell Art Museum in Fort Worth, Texas, a
classical art museum by Louis Kahn—the way the light defines
the spaces. More recently I was inspired by Peter Zumthor's
Kunsthaus Bregenz, and the Fondation Beyeler, outside Basel,
by Renzo Piano. The relationship of natural light and pure
space has always been inspiring for me. And I like Frank Gehry's
museums, including Bilbao—the excitement of exploring the
whole space, not just the white cubes.

*If you think of this story as a narrative, as an arc, where are we
now in the evolution of the museum form?*

We may have two extremes, one going toward the white cube
and another toward opening the cube, going out of the box. To
me, as an architect, exhibiting art does not necessitate white
cubes. For example, an exhibition could be in a forest. Or we
could explore something in between: being in nature but with

some architectural interventions. Something between nature and architecture could be an interesting space for art.

Let's talk about that space. Generally speaking, green space has been an afterthought for museums, except for the lucky few built in and around parks. That changed with Covid-19. As we speak today, in July 2022, the Uffizi in Florence has just announced the renovation of the Boboli Gardens. How is this connection becoming more prominent?
Of course, the pandemic was a reason to rethink those spaces. But to me green space, nature, is about something more. Nature is always changing, just as natural light is always changing. You experience each moment as something unique, different from the next. A white box or a black box is always the same. If the situation is always changing—as our life does—then you could experience art or space as a singularly precious moment. It would be great if artworks could have that kind of interactive relationship with each moment. No two experiences would be the same. The experience of art would not be controllable, in a sense.

And that seems to go against all the traditional impulses of museum design. Museums are usually super-controlled environments. Everything feels permanent, enclosed, defined. So how do you loosen up the museum with green space?
I think about gradations. It's not really about controlling and not controlling. It is about creating super-controlled situations, on the one hand, and then adding quite uncontrolled situations on the other hand. Some artworks really need delicately controlled situations, but others don't. Some can even be exposed to the elements. We can create diversities through gradations.

One boundary that many architects are now questioning is the one between spaces for art and spaces for sociability. How can they be softened up?
I like to bring the same ideas about gradation to this area. Whether a museum is in a park or in the city, the interaction between the inside of the museum and people's life activities is already happening. How can we make them blend together more and influence each other to make something better? That is the

Sou Fujimoto

point at which architecture can contribute something. Because real space always has these ambiguities. If you have one wall, then the inside and outside are clearly divided. But if you make two walls, or several walls with multiple openings, then we can blend the boundaries and create extra spaces between them.

I wonder what you think the impact of green space is on the actual experience of art. If you were to think of two museums with the same exact objects, one enclosed in concrete and the other in nature, how would that change the experience?
When the art museum is not like a box but more like open space, it can provide more freedom and inspiration for creative thinking. For visitors, it opens up diverse possibilities to perceive and understand the art. In a box, meaning feels definitive. Green or open space allows for different perceptions.

In some of your buildings the green space doesn't just surround the building—it is part of it. Trees poke holes through roofs; they grow inside. Tell me how you approach this dialogue of architecture and nature.
It depends on the situation. Nature is always different, place by place. I always carefully observe and listen. There is no single principle to apply, because I respect the diversity of nature. There is, of course, a great diversity of cultures and site conditions as well. Architectural design has to respect these situations and then try to invent the best, most amazing approach to suit each context.

How do you know you have found the right balance?
Honestly, we don't know exactly. We try our best. I try to find the fundamental essence of each project. We do many tests with models or renderings. We try out several different typologies. Some are interesting and some are not. And step by step, sometimes for practical reasons, sometimes for conceptual ones, we realize some of the ideas do not fit the situation. We continue until gradually we get closer and closer to the right point. At a certain point I feel a nice integration or harmony has been achieved between the functional requirements and

the site conditions and the visions for the future. If we had a hundred years to experiment, we would just keep going.

I assume there are all sorts of technical complexities involved in inserting plants this closely into buildings, with special requirements for air and condensation and bacteria. Can you tell me about some of these challenges—the things they don't teach you in architecture school?
In my time they certainly didn't tell you about any of this in architecture school. We collaborate with local landscape designers and professional tree experts. We have learned the proper size of the root and watering systems we need, and which species and in which seasons we can plant. We have achieved a basic level of knowledge, but we cannot understand everything. Each time we learn, and that is part of the excitement.

I loved visiting the classic gardens in Japan, especially those of the Moss Temple in Kyoto. Are there any principles of Japanese garden design that seem applicable to museums—that holistic sense of flow and asymmetry, for example?
All gardens, especially Japanese ones, are changing. The gardens of Kyoto were created three hundred years ago. They are different today from when they were designed. The gardeners have also changed their methods and knowledge. It is never a fixed design, but more like a dynamic fluidity of organic things. The acceptance of change is part of the heart of Japanese culture. At the Jingū complex in Ise, they demolish a shrine every twenty years and make it new, so what we see is quite recent but has nonetheless been continuing for thousands of years. While it is constantly changing, it is still fixed. That is the essence of the Japanese garden and of Japanese culture. And it is exciting to bring this thinking to the art museum. Because artistic creation itself is fluid, not static. It would be wonderful if the museum and the exhibition could keep changing, yet still somehow remain the same.

Serenity is a quality we associate with gardens, and sometimes museums. Many people go to museums for a sense of quiet and comfort. How should a museum feel?

I expect gradation in this respect, too. I don't expect a single quiet and calm situation, but I also don't expect only an active atmosphere. A museum should have places of calm along with zones of activity and noise. Then the total unity of all these features can feel like a city or a forest.

Is there an environmental message in your buildings?
I am probably not doing too much direct messaging about sustainability. Of course, this is now a central preoccupation. But I feel a more fundamental need to address how people perceive nature, how we can all live together with nature—which is not easy. Nature can be violent. We do need to control temperatures. What's important is to enjoy unexpected situations with nature as part of our lives. Of course, we have to do something about extreme heat or cold. But we can learn to live better together with nature. We can create a mindset so people can enjoy and accept natural conditions in their daily lives. Because fundamentally, nature is not controllable.

What other adaptations to nature will the future demand from museums?
I like to say that the art museum is where people will meet something unexpected. People should always get joy from the unexpected—then you yourself will change through the interaction with art and other people. And the same is true for nature. If you get close to nature, as with art, you will change. You will find new emotions, a new way of living. The art museum could be the place for such an encounter.

So, with all these ideas in mind, I would be curious to know how you would define a museum. What is it for you?
It is a place of diversity that can accept all different kinds of art activities and artworks, and all those different aspects of nature. Correspondingly, its architecture should not be like a strongbox, excluding something or defining something. It should be more of an open field of acceptance. A museum is a place for acceptance of diversities.

Do you get the feeling that some museums could have been better designed? What tends to frustrate you about them?

Some museums really force you to move in a specific way. They force you think a certain way. The architecture compels you to walk in one direction. I get uncomfortable when the violence of the building is too obvious. This doesn't mean classical museum buildings are not good. In fact, some of those big old buildings are quite flexible and well suited to being turned into a museum.

You are still young by architects' standards. What would be your dream project if any museum project could be yours?

A contemporary art museum is one, of course. At the same time, I am always thinking about integrating different aspects of our lives. I imagine designing a small city, not a crazy futuristic city, but more like a small community.

Normally, as architects we have site boundaries and then we make architecture. But for me, activities on the street and the connection between them and the landscape, all these in-between situations, are interesting. It would be great to design all of them into one strong concept. Such a totality would not usually be found in a building, but it could happen in a corner of a town. We could reorganize the street and the landscaping to create mixtures of architecture, landscaping, and urban life, with different programs working together. It would be lovely to design an entire small community this way.

I have asked many museum directors about their dream projects, and several of them said they would like to make an entire city into a museum.

That would be great.

We have had this lovely conversation about museums and a holistic green and human environment. Meanwhile, as we speak, huge fires are burning in the US and across Europe. How can museums help lead the way to a new relationship with our natural environment?

Recently it has been abnormally hot in Tokyo as well. I am an optimistic person, but when it comes to climate change I am less hopeful. People, including me, are too controlling of our living environment. We are too comfortable. We waste a lot of energy just to reduce the temperature of our rooms by one degree. Architectural construction is a huge industry. We must do something practical to survive. And we need to change our mindset, clearly, not just to solve problems but to accept situations of discomfort. Maybe this is where museums can play a role. Then we can start to enjoy life.

XU TIANTIAN
DnA Design and Architecture, Beijing

RURAL LIFE IS ITSELF A MUSEUM

In the picturesque village of Caizhai, nestled in the verdant hills of eastern China's Songyang county, visitors will come upon a surprising sight: a series of unabashedly modern wooden pavilions arrayed along the banks of a bubbling mountain stream. Functionally speaking, this is a tofu factory. But for Xu Tiantian, it's part of an experiment to revive interest in the rural life. Since 2013, the architect and her Beijing-based office, DnA, have completed twenty projects in Songyang, working closely with local officials and villagers. Some of the structures are designed to display objects, but most place the living practice of traditional crafts at the center. Customs and rituals become an occasion for shared experience. A recent project dispenses with built elements entirely, turning an abandoned stone quarry into a cultural space for the community. These "acupunctural" interventions are a means of reviving interest in a more traditional way of life, and they point to new possibilities for museums.

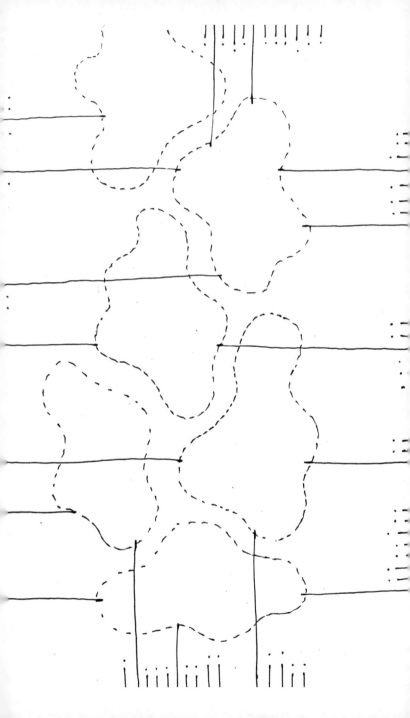

ANDRÁS SZÁNTÓ *You're not a typical architect. Your projects happen far away from the city, in rural and remote places. One of your recent projects transformed a series of open stone quarries in Jinyun County, in Zhejiang Province, into a cultural community space. What led to your interest in the rural life?*

XU TIANTIAN I agree, we are not mainstream architects. We work in a different format. The rural parts of China are different from our megacities. Many people feel that the rural world is the real China, where you can appreciate thousands of years of tradition. You can rediscover traces of the past. Rapid modernization and the urbanization process have made cities almost identical. People like me find a resonance in the rural regions.

I understand there is a rural renaissance in China. Meanwhile, China is still in the midst of the largest explosion of city-making in history. What drives this renewed interest in the rural life?

You can think of it as a policy from the government, but it is also a kind of reincarnation. People in cities are fed up with the hassles of urban life. In a rural region, you discover a different way of life. In our childhood, before urbanization, we still had that traditional way of living that is very similar to rural life. This renaissance brings people of our age and older back to the memory of the life they led before.

You have spoken about wanting to make buildings that are not iconic but more quiet. How?

I would compare our way of working to how artists work. We identify issues and initiate creativity. The architecture is a medium to revive a community, a village, a region. Our kind of architecture is not about showing off. It is to solve issues, to fix things, and restore local identity. That is part of the strategy. Iconic architecture in cities is mostly just about showing off. The dilemmas of rural regions require a different technique. This provides new possibilities for architects.

Are you working on any museums or cultural facilities right now?

We have been working with a number of cultural facilities in the rural regions. They are often a small village museum or a cultural center based on a highly specific program. For example, we may convert a local infrastructure facility into a water-conservancy museum. It depends how you define the word *museum*, really.

I'm curious—how do you define it?
I looked up the definition. It says that a museum is an institution to preserve heritage in a tangible way. But for me, it maybe is the opposite. Why not just give it all back to real life? If I had to put it in a short sentence, I would say that rural life is itself a museum. It is about maintaining (not preserving—that means it's frozen) and continuing that way of life.

Everything in rural China becomes a museum presentation. Everything seems to become a ceremony: how they produce things, how they cook the brown sugar, the emotion and atmosphere—it's all a beautiful performance. To me, this is a contemporary concept of the theater of the museum. That is why we speak of the intangible heritage of rural museums. Have you seen how they make tofu, or rice wine? Even the manual carving and excavating of the stone quarries are a form of ritual.

You trained at Harvard. You worked, briefly, for Rem Koolhaas at OMA. Koolhaas designed perhaps the quintessential iconic Western building in China, the CCTV headquarters in Beijing. It seems almost the opposite of what you are doing now.
You are absolutely right. I worked briefly for OMA. I discovered that I didn't like that way of working. When I returned to China, I worked briefly with the artist Ai Weiwei. That opened up a different world. Ai was collaborating with Herzog & de Meuron on the "bird's nest" National Stadium for the Beijing Olympics, but he was also building his own house and working with galleries. His architectural work has a different approach, and to me it was shocking. Seeing how artists are living and working also had a big impact on me. I am an architect—we are working with space—but like artists, we identify issues, diagnose symptoms, and then take architecture as a kind of medicine, as a treatment to provide a healing proposal to those symptoms.

China is where the most museums are being built worldwide today. Some are quite experimental architecturally. Some are deliberately trying to create a strong, iconic symbol for their cities. What has China brought to museum architecture, in your view?

Many projects in China are only about the architecture, the hardware—not the content, not the software. The rural museum is more about the content. It's about the village itself. The life there, the whole community, becomes an alternative museum. Architecture in this context doesn't have to be large or impressive. We speak of minimal intervention. We use the existing infrastructure. We can use live bamboo. This is the very opposite way of building museum architecture.

"Community" is a hot topic in museums everywhere. In a rural setting, it seems, community is everything.

In a city, "community" usually refers to the art community— the audience, the visitors, the tourists even. The city museum is institutional. It is not actually creating a direct dialogue with its local community, its neighborhood. In rural settings, the museum can be part of the strategy of restoring pride in and ownership of the local community. These museums become a public space for the villagers. Sometimes the museum is a production factory, a village factory—which is perfect. It becomes a kind of performance.

You have used the term acupuncture *to describe your process of making small interventions. It is a lovely metaphor. Civic institutions are a kind of acupuncture to bring a different energy to the life of the citizens. How do you go about administering this acupuncture approach?*

Acupuncture is not only about the needle spots. It is about stimulating the circulation. We are not talking about reviving one individual village; we are building up a region. Each village is given a rural museum, operated by that village. I want to clarify that the museum isn't the first priority in this approach. The idea is that a cultural facility belongs to the local community. The whole content is generated from and belongs to this village. This sense of ownership is really important.

Stylistically, understandably, your buildings incorporate local heritage. But they are also distinctively modern. How do you inject traditionalism in a balanced way, without turning it into kitsch?

This is always a discussion, on every project: whether it should be just a very authentic traditional building that really belongs to the past—what we call a fake antique—or whether it should be something iconic. Some villages want something iconic, like in the cities. There is always a fine line to walk between new and old. Our role in rural revitalization as architects is to form a kind of bridge. We provide a new possibility with our creative work, helping the community look to the future, but in a systemic, organic way. The building technique has to be local as well. We engage the villagers as contractors and builders.

Most architects do not make rural museums. I am interested in the implications of this outlook on museum architecture in general. If we can learn from Las Vegas, as Robert Venturi, Denise Scott Brown, and Steven Izenour suggested in their 1972 book, what are the lessons from rural China about making museums?

We have already learned so much from rural areas in the past years. We started with the villages, but we realized that in the urban centers there is still rural life under this thin veneer of urbanization. People have been living for four thousand years in rural communities, and they have preserved some of their way of living in the cities. Each neighborhood has its own history and legacy. We have been working in the urban context by introducing smaller-scale museums, each one with a specific program, like the Museum of Poetry or a Maritime Center. These museums really belong to the local community. For example, our Maritime Center is in an old shipyard with a history of more than a hundred years. The elders in this neighborhood can still talk about the good old days. The museum is bringing life back to its original source.

Who are your clients in these situations?

In the rural case, the local county government is the overall operator. We brought the initiative to the county government because it's rather a systematic strategy within the county region. Then each project has its own specific client. In the village it has to be the collective community. In the urban context it could be the cultural department or the transportation department. Working with them requires a lot of discussions, and during these conversations you get a better sense of what they need.

Thinking about big-city museums, what does museum architecture need to unlearn to adapt to the needs of society?
I don't deny the importance of these museums. They are a representation of our life and our culture. But for me, personally, I prefer what I call the life museum. It feels more lively or vivid to me. It has a deeper connection. And a rural museum, even with a tight budget and small scale, can contribute to improving the village revenue, and it can attract villagers to return home. It creates a social impact. Maybe the museum has more potential in this way.

There has been much talk recently about the "instrumental benefits" of cultural facilities—how they contribute to urban development or cultural tourism. Even so, the city has a huge ecology; it's hard to make a decisive impact there. Whereas in a small village, a museum can really make a difference.
Maybe the problem is that the function of the museum is too museum-like. Maybe it needs to open up and become more multifunctional. A museum should be an educational space, but it can also be a production space.

Talk to me more about the production spaces.
In the agricultural regions, each village has its own distinctive production. Along with the production of certain goods, the local culture has its own ceremonies, holidays, and festivals. The rice-wine factory or the brown-sugar factory is not just there to manufacture things. We create a venue to present the process of manufacturing as a form of live performance. We provide the architecture—the village museum—as a stage for this traditional production. In each village, the cooking masters become like characters on a stage. This respect for local production is something rare, and it is a treasure to the visitor from the city.

As such, it is also a strategy to increase the price of local goods and raise village revenues.

A wonderful amalgamation of culture and real life. I'd like to go back to your process. Once you are invited to work on a project, how do you come to a final design? These are not typical competitions, I assume.

No, they are not. Public projects that are within a certain budget don't have to go through competitions. We put forward these projects as a proposal to the local village community. As I mentioned, although I have been trained as an architect, I have worked with artists, and I appreciate how they initiate projects. I think this is the best way to work in rural communities. In most cases, we initiate. This is different from the conventional way of the architects receiving a commission.

Are the villagers surprised or startled by what you propose?

I would say it is a collaboration. It is not proposed to them as a surprise. After intensive communications, we come up with a proposal. You have to listen to their needs. You have to understand their realities, including the budget, the local way of seeing resources. If you can integrate that, then earning their approval becomes an easy step.

Has anything surprised you about their understanding of architecture? Have these interactions made you reassess your own training in architecture?

At first I was almost like a foreigner to the local context. When collaborating with the local builders, I felt so uneducated. I had little understanding of their building techniques. They know so much better what suits their local situation. There was a long learning phase for me. For the first year, we worked as pro bono advisors. I learned so much. That was my tuition.

Giving voice to members of the community is still rare.

The extreme case of the opposite would be starchitecture. You only read about the architects of those projects. But it's actually a collective collaboration, not just one person's job.

Your architecture, in searching for authenticity and local roots, is deeply concerned with materials. Wood. Stone. Bamboo. What role do materials play in your design process?
First of all, we look for anything handy, convenient for our project. It is very often recommended by the local villagers—whatever they have there, or whatever techniques they are familiar with. Material could be a metaphor. Our buildings are modern, but the material really delivers a message—it carries the cultural metaphor in these projects. That is what we like to work with, the cultural metaphor.

This connects to environmental consciousness. What message are these projects sending to mainstream museum design?
In a rural setting, culture is closely connected to agriculture. Before our industrial version, agriculture was closely tied to nature. In traditional culture there is deep respect for nature. Our culture has acknowledged biodiversity from ancient times, and this is simply forgotten in our industrial age. As architects, we learn from traditional wisdom. Local ways of building are low-budget and sustainable. That's why the stone quarry provides a new way of looking into architecture and public events.

Tell me more about the quarry project.
It was first intended as the ecological restoration of the interrupted landscape. At the same time, it's also intended to restore the sentimental connection with the local community. Even after having been abandoned for two decades, these quarries are still carrying memories of the thousand-year stone-mining history, which really shapes the local culture and character. We see our intervention in the quarry as an alternative architecture, a reevaluation of local resources—turning waste into a new type of public space that is closer to nature, not totally isolated or artificial, a space with more meanings and purposes.

And I assume the maintenance costs are low.
Yes, the total cost of safety reinforcement and space reuse is lower than with a new building. More importantly, all the projects in rural context require low maintenance. They work with

natural ventilation and natural lighting. Those are also ways of making the building more ecological.

I would like to come back to architecture as a form of healing. Some people look to museums for repair and solace. How can architecture create these moments?
The museum is a place that carries the memories of the individual or the collective. It is a reminder of the past, and that brings sentiments. Memory is part of the healing process for individuals. Knowing where you are from could indicate your future. That is very personal.

As the world changes—and China is changing rocket-fast— museums are rethinking their priorities. How do you see the role of the architect in this shifting context? What is it that architecture can do, and do uniquely?
It's not just that things are changing fast. We are in a critical moment in our history. We have a dilemma. We're kind of stuck. I had a meeting with a German architect earlier today. They were concerned about the war in Ukraine, and I complained about the lockdown here in China. There is a lot of pressure everywhere in the world. We have been thinking for the past two years about what we could do in the future. We want to make a constructive impact with our knowledge and our experience. There are so many more things architects can do around this world.

What would be your dream project, if any project could be yours?
I am currently working on my dream project! It is to reuse the abandoned *tulou* buildings in Fujian Province. These are large buildings with rammed earth walls, dating from the fourteenth century. They are a traditional form of housing built around a central courtyard for hundreds of people. There are thousands of abandoned *tulou* buildings in this area. This project also raises a new discussion about whether the traditional housing buildings could be revived and reused with adaptive modern functions and programs.

You teach architecture. Yet you practice an architecture that is very different from the kind of work most of your students will do. What advice would you have for a young architect who is aspiring to design museums to fit the future?

I want to encourage the younger generation to take initiative, to expand their perspectives and look for collaborations instead of waiting for projects to come to them. Architects are queuing up in cities, looking to do fancy projects. That's not the whole story of architecture, or of our capacity. We should find issues and use architecture to fix them, instead of just being a passive profession.

KUNLÉ ADEYEMI
NLÉ, Amsterdam & Lagos

AFRICA IS THE NEW MUSEUM

A floating museum? It would be possible in the architectural world of Kunlé Adeyemi, the forty-six-year-old
founder of NLÉ, which specializes in sensitive urban
interventions, especially in fast-growing African cities.
Born and raised in Nigeria, Adeyemi maintains offices
in Lagos and his home base in the Netherlands, where
he first got involved with museum design working
alongside Rem Koolhaas. Water, or more precisely the
building methods of people who are forced to live on it,
led Adeyemi to an epiphany about affordable and ecologically sustainable architecture. Africa has fostered
his appreciation for doing more with less and for
what he calls "human infrastructure." The continent
has lessons not just for the physical properties of
museums, but for their programming and organization
as well. For Adeyemi, a museum should be a place
of informality, flexibility, rootedness, and constant
surprise—with an architecture to match.

ANDRÁS SZÁNTÓ *Before launching your practice, NLÉ, in 2010, you worked with Rem Koolhaas at OMA on the Fondazione Prada in Milan and Leeum, Samsung Museum of Art in Seoul, among other projects. Were those your first museums?*

KUNLÉ ADEYEMI Yes. It was an illuminating time. I was fortunate to get that experience early on and to be in a position to lead a project. I was a very young architect to start in a large firm like OMA, and I just went straight into it. I began working on Leeum during my first years in the Netherlands. That project had begun many years before me, but we redesigned it completely.

You were born in Nigeria and studied architecture in the United States, at Princeton. But you ended up based in Amsterdam. Why?

I was born and raised in Nigeria, and attended the University of Lagos. I also had my first working experience in Nigeria for a couple of years, before moving to the Netherlands when I was twenty-five. I had lived there, working at OMA, for about nine years, before starting my practice, and that really gave me a degree of stability. The Netherlands created a hub that was important to my career path, which has always been globally focused. Amsterdam is accessible to all of Europe, America, Africa, Asia. I continue to spend a lot of time in Africa, especially Nigeria, where a lot of my interests, passion, and focus still remain.

How has your connection with African heritage informed your thinking about the purposes, materials, and attitude of architectural design?

In Africa, there is still a lot of what one could refer to as "green"—not green as a color, but in the sense of being untouched, natural, raw. You come to understand that you need very little to survive or even develop in any environment. I was raised in Kaduna, in northern Nigeria. It is a landlocked city. A river runs through it. It's a very green and natural environment. My father cultivated the land around us; we had a farm and some animals. My father, being an architect, created our home. So I lived in a contemporary house in a suburban area, but also had that experience of living on a farm. Being so close to the land has really shaped my thinking about development. I know from my upbringing that we only need a minimal amount of restructuring of the natural environment to coexist with it.

Another influence the African context had on me is the informality and the people, how they interact with one another and with social structures. That interaction is casual and family-oriented. And being raised in areas where I have seen people thrive with scarce resources has really shaped my own way of thinking. I have observed that in other parts of the Global South as well. You learn to create maximum impact with minimum resources.

Africa, with its rapid development, could become a real laboratory for the museum. What does the African context bring to the discourse around the museum?
Africa as a region is too large to generalize about. But when you go into some parts of Africa, the kinds of works and investigations and relationships and social opportunities you find are very much aligned with what museums nowadays aspire to be. In that sense, one could argue that from the point of view of social interaction and innovation and creativity, Africa is the new museum. There is just so much happening on the continent. Perhaps Africa provides an opportunity to rethink the structure of museums, not just as physical spaces but as cultural institutions.

Do you see an opening up of the model as the museum moves farther from its roots in the Global North?
Absolutely. And that potential plurality is most evident in the African context, where there is so much cultural diversity. I wouldn't say this is particular to Africa alone. But what a lot of museums aspire to create now, you literally find on the streets of many parts of Africa—these unscripted, out-of-this-world experiences. There is still space for surprises within these cities and communities. The question is, how do we capture that narrative, and in what formats can this be called a museum?

The need to explain what a museum does to people who haven't been to a museum before has led to some incredibly inspirational practices in Africa. So in a curious way, the continent with the fewest so-called museums may point to the museum's future.

Kunlé Adeyemi

The question becomes: How do we redefine the format? The museum has always been closely linked to a particular spatial construct, and it seems difficult to disconnect that spatial construct from the program and functions of the museum. Maybe it is hard to create a museum without such a spatial construct. Would it lose its value? Can we redefine a museum without that familiar spatial experience? There is a fear within the institution about taking that step. Only very contemporary museums seem to be able to do it. And the more they do, the more they are disqualified from being seen as museums. They are considered a mere "cultural center" or a "multipurpose space."

Before we go on, I want to touch on your deep connection to water. A renowned project of yours was a floating school. You have worked on water-based architecture as a solution for cities. Can you briefly tell me about the source of this fascination for you?
It all began when I was researching affordable housing, around 2010–11. We decided to find out how people build the cheapest dwellings in Lagos. If you can understand how they do it, maybe you can find more than just a hypothetical idea of what housing should be. It occurred to me that people who live in the community of Makoko, a community with thousands of timber-framed structures sitting on stilts in the water, can offer solutions for lightweight construction. The building system there is fast, economical, made by hand. They are building on water, which in many parts of the world is not considered real estate. I learned from people who had built hundreds of those homes. The houses were more or less replicable, modular. They followed a typology that was very different from what was built on land, and it had been completely overlooked by the city. These guys have been building this way for hundreds of years, through trial and error. There is a lot to learn from them.

Who knows, maybe one day we'll see a floating museum?
Could be, yes, on water. The community of Makoko is, in a way, itself a floating museum. It is a place you go and learn. There is so much to see, to uncover, so much history, so many insights into the future. In July 2011, just as we were doing this research, there was a huge rainstorm, and the entire city of Lagos was

flooded. I realized that when we think we are buying land, we are actually just buying water. This was an epiphany for me. Lagos is one of the fastest-sinking cities in the world. We are on a collision course between two challenges, urbanization and climate change.

Let's go back to your understanding of museums. Do you look to any particular buildings or projects as icons of museum design?
Frank Gehry's Guggenheim Bilbao undeniably had an impact on me as a young architect—seeing a space that was so different not only materially, but also spatially. Museums take you on a journey through space as you experience the content—for instance, Frank Lloyd Wright's Guggenheim takes you on that spiraling journey. In a successful museum, you always feel the power of space. And natural environments can offer that same powerful experience. In Saudi Arabia a few years ago, I had some mind-blowing spatial experiences in the ancient natural landscape. Nature may be the best form of a museum.

Thinking about Bilbao and that striking architectural state-ment—the museum as a work of art—I do wonder: Are we still there, or have we moved on?
I would hope that we are moving on, not by abandoning that as a way of producing museums alone, but as a way of expanding the narrative. We have to realize that we have in many environments all the infrastructure we need to tell stories. So it's about shifting our focus. I wouldn't say, "Let's never build another museum as a spatial construct." But it is no longer enough to produce space just for the sake of awe. We have to do alot more.

Given all that, how would you define a museum?
I think a museum is an environment that holds history, pro-motes the present, and sees the future.

There are many challenges involved in realizing this kind of museum, for today and for the future. Through much of history, museums were designed for paintings and sculptures. Today's art involves many more mediums. How do you create the right kind of spaces for it?

Kunlé Adeyemi

There is a need to deconstruct the traditional spatial typology. And the more we unpack the expanded definition of the museum, the more we can integrate the museum into the city and the surroundings as well. This requires flexibility, and that is an approach a lot of architects try to build into their projects. However, flexibility sometimes yields a lack of clarity, unfortunately. The building becomes so generic that it lacks specificity.

Above all, the museum must respond to the present, which embodies both the past and the future. The museum of the future is already in the present. We have to understand this specific context—the demographics, the economy, the social politics, the infrastructure, the morphology of the site, the available resources—to define the appropriate museum experience.

Most people live in cities now, so architects have to understand and respond to the city. Your practice is deeply rooted in urbanism. You have worked on master plans for vast urban projects. NLÉ has a research arm working to analyze urban-rural transformation. What is its philosophy?
Urbanization and climate change are the two key pillars that define social development. We break them down further, into what we call the seven factors of development, for which we have an acronym, *DESIMER:* demographics, economics, social politics, infrastructure, morphology, environment, and resources. By analyzing these factors, we can understand the urban dynamics of any context we are dealing with.

How would this research method play out when thinking about a museum in a particular urban situation, let's say in Lagos?
First we would try to understand the critical ideology behind the institution. We would speak with experts in the industry, the thought leaders, to understand their positions and to situate the institution historically. Then we would analyze Lagos, which is an incredibly dynamic city. It is said to be the largest city in Africa, with over 15 million people. It is perhaps the largest economy in Africa, so there is a lot to learn from the economic positioning of Lagos. We can continue down that line to look at social politics. The question we would be looking to answer is how to weave those insights into an experience, and define it as a museum.

As a strategist, I like this holistic approach; it's like a funnel. You have written about the Global South and a condition you describe as "urban crawl." What challenges will face the museums of tomorrow's megacities?

The challenges are spaces of opportunity for the narrative of the museum. The museum is well positioned to highlight these challenges, which ultimately define the qualities of such cities. Of course, there are challenges of infrastructure, to take one of those DESIMER factors, and the infrastructure for the production of a museum in the Global South is lacking. But it is also the question of how you define the necessary infrastructure. There is certainly a scarcity of physical infrastructure, from the standpoint of conventional museums. But there is an abundance of human and social infrastructure.

What do you mean by human and social infrastructure?

Infrastructure is an enabler of any kind of activity. Typically, we envisage these as physical enablers, such as buildings or equipment. But human connections and relationships—the social network—can also make things move ahead. That was part of my definition of urban crawl. There is a certain point at which the agglomeration of people reaches a threshold where the sum of the individual parts starts to behave as a whole. People start to swarm and move in similar ways, giving rise to a sort of collective intelligence. And that collective intelligence is an incredible human infrastructure, which produces surprising results.

Cities like Lagos are chaotic, but somehow there is an inherent order in that chaos. Collective human infrastructure, collective human intelligence, comes together. Lagos thrives. It is constantly developing and moving, regardless of its poor physical infrastructure. It has developed its own social infrastructure.

Perhaps harnessing human infrastructure and collective intelligence could be an interesting way to define the museum. But one thing we know is that those megacities of the future are alienating. They sever family ties and traditional ways of community-centered living. Can museum architecture provide a kind of new gathering space?

Kunlé Adeyemi

For sure. I imagine that would be one of the most important goals of museum architecture, to foster community spaces and development, and indeed to enhance the collective experience. Museums have done well by providing places that go beyond just being destinations for spectacle. They can and do foster community interaction. This is why architecture for us is not just about the design of space. It is really a tool to orchestrate these complex urban dynamics.

Let's talk about the climate side of the equation. We all have a rough sense of the climate conditions people will face in the future. It's a slow-moving train crash. Knowing what's coming, what are some implications for architecture, and for museum architecture specifically?
Let's learn from history. Let's look at how humanity has adapted and survived, and let's learn from our biological and ecological histories. That could be a mandate for how the museum can deal with this climate future. There have been times in history when temperatures have risen, dropped; there have been floods, fires, etc. And people have lived through those moments. There is a lot to learn, including from the mistakes we made back then, so as to not repeat them.

Museums tend to be large, energy-consuming buildings. Can there be more of a circular economy for museum buildings?
You are right, museums are mostly hermetic spaces in many parts of the world, because of the nature of the artifacts they tend to preserve. They need to be insulated from the external environment and that, fundamentally, is energy-consuming. We have to deconstruct that concept to become more energy-efficient. How can you reconnect the museum space to its natural environment? That could mean having more open space or creating spaces that are more energy-efficient in their design. Ultimately, we need to rethink the museum as a hermetically sealed space that holds things that are almost alien to their immediate environment.

Meanwhile, everybody is talking about the metaverse and digital spaces. What do you make of all that?

We are all becoming more connected with our digital environment. Virtual museums and entertainment spaces are not going away anytime soon. But does that eliminate the need for physical environments? Absolutely not. Does it heighten the need for more physical environments? Yes. Right now, we are creating more and more virtual interfaces with our physical selves. But this heightens our need to create a more tactile, present, really more connected world. I don't think there is a fear of the digital being a threat to our humanity. It will just make it more versatile.

What would be a dream museum project for you?

A dream museum would revolve around the themes we have been discussing. A museum that tackles environmental issues and climate impacts. A museum that deals with new cultures in the changing urban and climatic conditions we are living in. I don't know yet how that would be framed. But I would love to get a brief that challenges us to think about those issues and create a museum experience around them.

I would like to close on the idea that architects are agents of change. But what exactly is the change that architects, specifically museum architects, should or could promote?

I think that change is evident. It has to do with the changes that have an impact on our adaptation as a human species, the changes that we can embody socially, culturally, and economically that would enable us to survive and evolve as a species. That really starts with creating conditions that allow us to think differently, to build differently, and ultimately, to live differently.

Kunlé Adeyemi

WINY MAAS
MVRDV, Rotterdam, Shanghai, Paris, Berlin

A GIANT LABORATORY OF THINGS WAITING TO BE EXPLORED AND DISCOVERED

Just as I was starting work on this book, the Museum Boijmans Van Beuningen, in the Dutch port city of Rotterdam, opened a revolutionary annex billed as the world's first publicly accessible art-storage facility. Covered in reflective glass and perched high above the ground—and future rising sea levels—the Depot, as it is called, provides unfettered access to the museum's 151,000-object collection, while allowing behind-the-scenes glimpses of its conservation and research activities. Containing fourteen storage compartments and five climate zones, the Depot's bulbous interior is not just visually striking. It also seriously challenges conventional museum-making. It hands over agency to the visitors, who can design their own pathways through the collections and view objects at will. This new approach stems from the imagination of Winy Maas and his colleagues at MVRDV, a practice devoted to building "innovative, social, green, realistic, and remarkable architecture for a changing world."

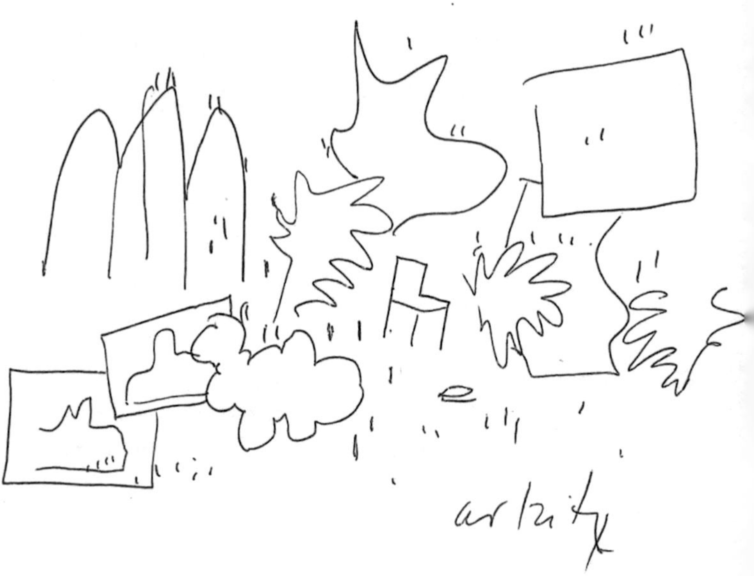

ANDRÁS SZÁNTÓ *We must begin with a project you completed not long ago. The Depot Boijmans Van Beuningen is a message about the future. How did it come about?*

WINY MAAS A decade ago there was a flood in Rotterdam. A lot of the paintings in the underground storage of the Boijmans Museum were under threat. Some got wet. It was a sign to make a new building. At that time, while visiting the Schaulager in Basel—designed by Herzog & de Meuron—with Sjarel Ex, the director of the Boijmans Museum, we were imagining how an open, public storage building would give more meaning to a museum. It started there: the idea that everybody could see the more than 90 percent of what is normally hidden. The collection would be more widely celebrated by the audience.

We suggested bringing the Depot into the city instead of the periphery. Such a public depot could not be a black enclosed box. Opening it to a public would require more security, climate protection, staff—more budget. This led to a brief for this new kind of institution: a combination of storage and public access. We won the competition with the design as it stands now.

The building challenges how museums operate. You're handing over power to the visitor even while solving the problem of storage.

We proposed a couple of things. We positioned curatorial work next to archiving. We worked on hospitality. Normally, an archive is for researchers: They sit in a corner, they ask for a piece, it comes to them. We suggested creating a maximum amount of in-between places, so visitors can pull out objects and see them in groups—for example, all the Picassos. We activated in-between spaces—we call them galleries—allowing for flexibility and neutrality. And light. We added an atrium where art can be shown. We added a garden on the roof, also to exhibit works outdoors, and a plaza below, for the same reason. All of which allows many different ways of looking. We can call it maybe a democratic way of looking, using your own choices.

The museum next door is classical white. It is curated from historical, personal, or socio-economic perspectives. Not this building. The Depot is gray and utilitarian everywhere, to avoid this whiteness and address the view. It has a cold light system, which we developed with Philips, and which turned out cool. In the gray environment, it feels almost like you are in a mine that opens up toward the top. You love it after a while. After half a year of the Depot being open, the institute is developing the hospitalities by adding tours. I know there are more ways of dealing with a depot. This is a start. It opens up a journey for architects and institutions to follow.

You set up MVRDV with Jacob van Rijs and Nathalie de Vries in 1993. What have you learned from projects you did before that you can now bring to museums?
I am a landscape architect and an urbanist. One element in landscape architecture is time. Landscape architects know that things grow, flourish over time. And landscape is about the overview, the panorama—which much of architecture lacks. This helps to position our work. Those notions can be found in many of our projects. We applied that, and also learned from, for instance, our work on libraries, like Book Mountain in Spijkenisse, in the Netherlands, which shows the collection A-to-Z. At the Brabant Library, in the south of the Netherlands, we were making a complete A–Z sorter, an instrument to understand the tremendous (bio)diversity of human knowledge.

For François Pinault's art collection, in Île Seguin, we proposed an "art mixer." This would not have been a static museum. Each room would be able to change and adapt in seconds or minutes, shifting color and light, dimensions and directions—to show artworks in specific ways. It would have been like a huge "tile," a 100-by-100-meter horizontal building with rails in the roofs and the floors. A robot would orchestrate how these rooms moved, like a Rubik's Cube. Pinault in the end stopped the project and moved on to establish the Pinault Collection in the Bourse de Commerce, in Paris, with Tadao Ando. I still love the concept of the art mixer.

Your firm's motto is "We create happy and adventurous places." You talk about "spaces that make you smile." Can museums make people smile?
A radical art mixer for sure would make you smile. Why? Because you would see the transformer endlessly working.

For some people it would be a nightmare; for others, a smile. You cannot guarantee smiles for everybody. I like to position architecture in such a way that it pushes what already exists and looks to the future, questioning tradition. An art mixer does exactly that. It's futuristic. It's incredibly beautiful.

What can actual museums do to become more happy and adventurous places? What do they need to unlearn?
The neutrality of many museums is understandable, but also a burden. Square rooms with light from above, interrelated in a certain way—and that's it. This is a convenient way of showing the work of artists and curators. These spaces are based on a common denominator: the average size of an artwork and the need for four to five meters around each visitor. Such standardization is an incredible optimized tool for museums to exhibit art. It has developed over a century. I won't say it's bad. But it does lack something: bigness, interaction, surprises, challenges.

I celebrate (bio)diversity—of people, animals, plants, architecture, and cities. I see architecture as a means of making the world somehow bigger. Art and architecture both do that, and the combination of the two makes it even more interesting and profound. Art comments on and criticizes us. It cheers us up, and it gives us space for escape.

Making the world bigger is a lovely definition of art. But how would you define a museum?
A super-good question. The museum is a library, on the one hand. A museum is, for me, also an escape out of the real world, somehow. It is a place for contemplation and inspiration, for sure. It is a place that reflects, in a conceptual way, on our times and our reality. It is not predictable like Walt Disney World theme parks, and it shouldn't be. It is also a platform for meeting art and thinkers. And it should be a place full of surprises.

So let's talk about your notion of the "new old." Artists are constantly making new work. What are we to do?
Let's start with the beauty of that amazing collection that humankind already made, and its function. We want to store and protect things that can disappear, that are rare and

precious. All museums, put together, are pieces of our collective consciousness. They are the ultimate celebration of mankind, together with all its cultural flaws. Humankind's collection is huge, and over time endless. And it all starts with questions: Do we want to store this object? Do we want to keep it? Do we see it as a treasure?

We have a growing population and artists who are endlessly producing new works. They are creating a sort of "new old." Meanwhile, almost every human being has in his or her house a collection—pottery, or paintings, writings, books. But for sure we reach a point of insanity. It's insane to keep all this stuff. Nowadays there are people who are deciding to keep almost nothing, who live in tiny homes, in a nomadic way, to reduce possessions. This is a good moment in time to reflect on what we should keep and how and where.

As we move into the metaverse, as some suggest, there will be a yearning for the patina of the real. For the moment that battle is balanced. Fifty years from now, the virtual world will take over more. For now, there remains a huge role for heritage, for personal experience as it is reflected in paintings or sculptures. The internet is a partial solution to engaging the vast collection of humanity. But open-data centers for art are not yet well developed. How are we to give access to all this art and art data—to the "Depot Plus"? I don't have an answer yet. Maybe a specialist like you would know where we could find this ultimate Noah's Ark of art, or perhaps a collective of museums.

That Noah's Ark needs a client. To make the Depot, you also needed a client that was willing to play along. What makes a good client?
A good client thinks about the future. A good client has knowledge of what he or she wants, but also respect for others who surround them with advice and authenticity. It's always interesting to find how the client wants to make or develop a visionary statement.

I'm curious, how do you go about designing a cultural facility "for maximum happiness for their users," to use your words?
By listening. Observing the context. For the Depot, the context was the contemporary art world. I try to make each project different, for (bio)diversity. Every site on the planet is different, and every client is different. For example, we are making an art gallery for a private collection in the Netherlands. Our client has a beautiful collection, in the dunes. You cannot build there; you must go underground. So we created a gallery frame, a linear narrative of the collection, which forms the word *EVA*, visible from the sky—it's the name of the collector's wife. I find that so personal, so distinct. The collector buried this collection for his wife. I'm touched by that. It is a vulnerable piece of architecture. Architecture becomes a story.

People in the museum field are pushing for a more community-minded, transparent, engaged institution—a new software for the museum. How can architecture lead the way?
One way is content and quality. And intricacy. When you raise curiosity, you attract people. Then there will be a higher potential for engagement. The next element is what I would call contemporariness and future. That resonates with people. What are we dealing with these days? What worries us? Those questions should be triggered by a museum. That's partly about the programming, but architecture can facilitate.

Are there good examples?
There are. The Tate Modern's Turbine Hall is a beautiful example—not only the hall, but how it is programmed. Olafur Eliasson's *Little Sun* had an outstanding combination of intricacy, drama, monumentality, and contemporariness. I love the factory model of the Centre Pompidou. It was the best work Renzo Piano ever made, because of its contrasts and how it creates a desire to go inside. It was courageous to position it this way, like a horizontal Eiffel Tower—an intelligent and intricate answer to what a museum can be. I love the Kunsthal Rotterdam, Rem Koolhaas's masterpiece, a kind of *promenade architecturale*. You can walk through it and always find intricacy and surprise.

So how will tomorrow's museums look and feel different? What will surprise us about them?

There is a difference between programming and architecture, but one can blend the two, as with the art mixer, and that's what I would love to see more of in the near future. Another element is the intelligent weirdness of spaces. I can imagine a giant laboratory of things waiting to be explored and discovered. The opportunity is to make new museums with endless invention that help draw people in. Whatever the solution, it has to be intelligent. I respect the Centre Pompidou and the Kunsthal because they still keep inspiring architects to invent.

Are you involved in any metaverse projects? What are your thoughts about online environments for art?

I am involved in a couple. For me, the metaverse is like an anti-city, the alter-ego of society. It's not very culturally driven—yet. It is very commercial. The architecture looks exactly like what we have in the real world, in order to calm the potential users. For me it can be a place for reflection on what we are not building yet. The metaverse could be an extension of the public museum. Ultimately urbanism, too, should take place in the metaverse. It's an adventure at the moment to imagine what the metaverse design should be and what may come out of this enterprise. We haven't reached the tipping point, but being inside a digital space will eventually become somehow normal.

Let's turn to ecology. You have advocated for creating what you call a "sponge," a kind of ever-changing green layer over our cities. How does this apply to museums?

We envision a *new nature* that covers and embodies our cities, open and porous, flexible and biological, sheltering our planet, providing shadow and cooling and processing food and water. It will take a while before we have buildings and cities that are completely biological, organic, recyclable; where materials can deteriorate or grow; where bird nests are as important as human buildings; where intelligent organic design that is flexible and creates shelters on the go is being applied. That *new nature* looks like a green sponge that shelters the users, protects the planet, keeps the water, adds cooling. We are working on it in different ways. In Dubai, by working on a mall without air conditioning. In the Netherlands, by working on wooden pixels to make fully adaptable wooden buildings. We are imagining organic materials that can adapt to you, forming a second skin around you when you need it, like a jungle that surrounds you. That's the kind of city I would like to find myself in.

So how does a museum fit into that? That transformative biological world for sure will lead to other ways of making and storing art. There are already tendencies in art that offer glimpses: highly digitized works that appear whenever you want, sculptures that are made and reproduced as we speak. I don't know if that is a world gallerists and museums would be happy with. I know this is a far-fetched dream, but it cannot be denied.

Now you have definitely taken us into the future. You really are a Noah's Ark person.
If you go to the future in your spaceship, when you come from Mars, maybe you won't see a blue planet but a green planet. It's a hypothesis, I know, but I am beguiled by it. It's true: It is a Noah's Ark version of the future, and the planet itself is the ark. I try to approach it like Alexander von Humboldt, to become systematic. The works of Humboldt show the determination of the complexity of that ark.

Let's come back to the now. Many people are put off by museums. Does the shiny architecture put people off?
With the word *shiny*, do you refer to the mirroring of the Depot? Or to the tech-end high buildings of the past twenty years?

I was referring to the attention-grabbing buildings people associate with starchitecture. But let's keep talking about the Depot.
Architecture is a tool. I'm pretty aware that the Depot building, which is in fact a mirror, could be considered distant. But a depot cannot be transparent, due to climatic and security constraints. By reflecting the environment, it makes you, the park, and the city bigger. It gives back a reflective space, or a space for reflection. That intrigues people. It is too soon to know if all people love it, but as we speak people are embracing

it as an architectural gesture. Helping the public to appreciate these treasures makes the collection more sustainable and long-lasting.

There are many interesting new demands being placed on museums. Some look to museums for healing, repair, solace. How can architecture create such healing moments?
That is part of our profession. We have to provide buildings that repair the mistakes we have made. The Depot repairs the park. It repairs the seclusion of our collective archives. This has to be combined with spaces where you want to be. There are critics who say if the architect doesn't want to live in the house (s)he designs, then (s)he should be punished. I feel that I make buildings where I want to live, to stay, to reflect. I think contemplation is key. Art is contemplative. Architecture has to help that sometimes. The museum can be a contemplative space. Those are my interpretations of the words *healing* and *wellness* that you are offering.

What tools help people achieve this warm, contemplative state?
In general, museums are often made of stone and white surfaces, to make space for art and artists. It has to do with what and how artists want to show, and also with the size of today's art. Actually, it's a tendency that comes to us from the painters of the Renaissance. It is still in our brain as the required format for presenting art. However, a constantly changing, biological, contemplative environment will challenge our existing notions of art. Can I forget all the concrete and the stone? Do I need to be so neutral? Or ultimately is it all only for the art market? I like interventions by artists. I love events like Manifesta that explore where art is going. We will have to test these assumptions to get to the next level in our thinking about art and its institutions.

You once quoted the poet Paul Éluard, who said, "There is another world and it is in this one." This is a statement of hope. It suggests that we can somehow hack the existing world in order to get to a better one. How can architecture expose that better world hiding inside this one?

Through slight changes that can reveal progress on a larger scale. By showing that a brick can be a brick that changes into something else. By showing the seeds of change. I am thinking of our Crystal Houses, in Amsterdam, where the bricks and lintels are made of glass. They suggest that the old can become new. And they have helped Amsterdam accept a modernity within. A Trojan horse. It's a dream about ultimate transparency. That is how you hack the current situation. You change a little bit of the DNA of what we know, and that leads us into this new world.

KABAGE KARANJA & STELLA MUTEGI
Cave_bureau, Nairobi

THINGS ARE GOING TO GO FULL CIRCLE

On a hot summer afternoon in 2022, I found myself at Columbia University's Graduate School of Architecture, in a crit session run by Kabage Karanja and Stella Mutegi, founding partners of the Nairobi-based Cave_bureau. The students had just concluded a semester devoted to exploring how the subterranean landscape of natural caves and abandoned man-made infrastructure might offer innovative solutions for urban and environmental resilience in New York City. The projects, including one that envisioned a museum in a derelict subway tunnel, were breathtakingly original. For Karanja and Mutegi, Africa is the perfect launching pad for these ideas. The museum on the continent is inextricably linked to histories of colonial erasure and extraction. Yet Africa is poised to become a laboratory for museum-making. The cave—both as physical space and as metaphor—is a provocation to test the limits of contemporary architecture. It invites new thinking about how the museum can adapt to a more community-focused, ecologically sensitive, low-carbon future.

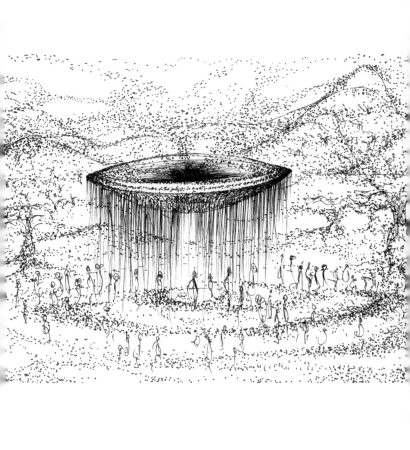

ANDRÁS SZÁNTÓ *You are unusual participants in this book. While you have done a lot of thinking about museology, you have not designed a brick-and-mortar museum, at least not yet. How did your partnership come about?*

STELLA MUTEGI We were fired on the same day. We worked together in a big architectural firm. They were laying people off, and we happened to be among those being let go. We went our separate ways, but a few months later we got in touch, and Cave was born.

Your official titles are Matri(arch) and Explorer, respectively—not your typical designations in an architecture studio. Can you elaborate?

SM Many young people come to work at Cave with a lot of unlearning to do. Apart from guiding them in their professional careers as architects and researchers, I am also the mother hen in the office. I ask tough questions. I'll expect an answer, and I will not move on until I get one.

KABAGE KARANJA: I am an explorer because I have always taken an interest in going out into the wild. One of my first, most visceral experiences was sleeping in a cave. That framed my philosophy of looking into caves. I do a lot of hunting and thinking about opportunities for us. I bring them to the office and put them on the table with our Matriarch, Stella, and we decide what's worth pursuing.

Your core interest is the anthropological and geological context of the post-colonial African city. What are your observations on the museum, especially the art museum, in the African context?

SM The museum in Africa is problematic. It is an installation of what the colonialists thought the museum should be. Culturally, Africans didn't have museums per se. We had artifacts, rituals, and objects, which were not intended for display. We didn't necessarily exhibit things for pleasure or for study. From a colonial point of view, these were alien things of interest to share with others, and this meant displaying them and writing about them. A museum is almost alien to Africa.

KK The contents and practice of museology have been even more problematic from the colonial perspective. They are extractive. The museum is not an innocuous, harmless institution where beautiful objects are simply displayed. Museums have used modes of erasure along the way. It was about de-civilization and conquest, as aptly described by Kathryn Yousoff in her 2019 book *A Billion Black Anthropocenes or None*. Our equivalent of the museum was more in tune with life and the appreciation of real-time existence, where children were taught what it meant to live in an actual environment and in a community setting. At Cave, we focus on that real-life enactment of practice within Indigenous spaces.

An emphasis on social gathering is a current preoccupation for museums. So this may be a case where Indigenous ideas can be re-integrated. What do you think?
KK We feel things are going to go full circle. Following the pandemic and given the pressures of environmental destruction, it makes perfect sense for institutions to look at Indigenous practices as new knowledge-making centers, to rethink this so-called civilization. We need to reassess our modes of existence.

Tell me about the cave as a metaphor, as a set of ideas.
SM You can go back to the cave and start again. The cave was shelter for early man and a space of life expression across stone walls. The cave for us, in the colonial context, was a place where we went back to reclaim our lands, our freedom. It is the place we go back to so we may forge our way into the future—a place of refuge, of refreshment, of origin.

In this century, the museum seems poised to proliferate on the African continent. How might that fractalize our view of the museum?
KK The architect, author, and curator Lesley Lokko has said that Africa is the laboratory of the future. It has the youngest population in the world. There are exciting movements and modes of interaction that will embody new thoughts about what a museum is, should be, can be.
SM Many institutions right now have to grapple with whether they have the moral authority to display the objects in their vast collections. They are questioning how they got them and whether they should return some of them. There is going to be a big shift.

About the Anthropocene Museum, you have written that it is "an institution of creative action, not constrained by four walls, but generative enough to openly challenge the prevailing status quo— literally from the ground up."[1] What are the implications?
SM We call it a roaming museum. We tackle a different issue in every place we have been, such as colonialism or climate change. These are uncomfortable subjects, and for a long time they have been buried. To put it simply: The Anthropocene Museum is an awareness museum that brings to the fore issues that are not comfortable, that require deep discussion and new frameworks to be put in place to resolve.

Kabage, what does it mean for you?
KK The geological grounding and basis of our thinking are what frames the hardware of the museum. In our Anthropocene Museum 1.0, we were in Mount Suswa, an active volcano in Kenya along the Great Rift Valley. We examined the practice of extracting geothermal power from the ground. The government of Kenya and international organizations such as the World Bank and United Nations have been complicit in sidelining the local Indigenous people from the benefits of this project. We bring to light these problems. We made installations to talk to the communities within the caves about issues surrounding geothermal energy. It is important for museums to be a lens on culture and society, to question complicated issues that impact the natural environment and the people that live there.

I like the image of the museum as lens. In a 2008 article, you talk about "liberating and cerebral spaces of refuge that our freedom- fighting forebears inhabited, in particular, caves."[2] This is an African heritage. What can institutions worldwide take away from this line of thinking?
KK People are at the heart of what we do. And people are usu- ally marginalized within the prevailing discourse, including discussions about art and culture. We find it valuable to have discussions with communities that are often left by the wayside in mainstream cultural debates. That would be the takeaway: that at heart, it's not about following the latest trends within any curatorial program. As Amitav Ghosh has said, the climate

crisis is also a crisis of culture, and thus of the imagination. Museums have been, and often still are, problematic players in the Anthropocene, compounding the state of crisis in the world today. Here we simply return instinctively back to caves as our decolonial freedom-fighter ancestors did, to continue reimagining the African state of the future.

How do you situate the efforts of architects to embed the museum in an African context?
SM They are a bit problematic. These architects are re-creating something that is already problematic. Putting up a building is not the way forward. We need to find creative ways of curating, especially coming from the African context, where much of our history was oral, passed down from generation to generation. A good basis to start would be understanding that a museum in Africa cannot be a fancy building that is going to win you awards.

Kabage, do you agree that you can't really have conventional museum buildings in Africa—or only with different intentions and modalities?
KK We can, and we will. But for now, we still seem to be using the same software to think about the institution, and it is conjoined to the same hardware, the building. Yes, museums are rethinking how they can be constructed closer to the community—and that is great. But the same economics are at play, and private patrons are financing the museum if the government is not interested, which is the reality in most of Africa. And the private sector is not immune to compromise.

Physical structures are needed in the context of restitution of heritage artifacts. The Benin Bronzes are headed back to Benin City after spending more than a century dispersed across various European and American museums, partly because new museum infrastructure is being built for them. How do you see this process playing out?
SM It is good to acknowledge that these things are being returned. But they are being returned to a different context—to people who might find them alien, because there has been so

much erasure of culture. Do you put them in a museum? Do you give them back to the community they were taken from? Do those people still value these objects? That is a huge dilemma facing these institutions.

KK It should be said that the artifact-restitution process is still fraught with delay tactics, bad faith, and more than not, condescending bravado. The communities that were directly affected are rarely if ever brought to the table to plan this return, which we term as a disjointed process of reverse curation. Again, we see here the colonial machinery at work, sidelining the primary curators of these artifacts, who have the right to decide what they do or don't do with these stolen goods inside or indeed outside the confining walls of the museum building.

Let's talk about administrative structures. These are likewise legacy elements. How would you redefine the roles of a curator or director? What new roles might have to be invented?

KK I will give you an example. At Mount Suswa, we deal with a conservationist called Ishmael. His knowledge about the geography of the site goes beyond anything we have experienced, as do his sensitivity and closeness to the community. Museums are in no way even in touch with such an individual. You almost wonder: Should the institution remain as it is, and then have such agents who can apply pressure on the institution? Or should the institution be broken up and dispersed into the community, a sort of devolution of its operation, so it can then begin to express what it is about in the context of what is important to them?

Architecturally, materially, spatially—what would such an institution look like?

KK We gravitated to caves because they are spaces already being used by the community. The people aren't mobilized enough to curate exhibitions in the caves, but there are many caves where this could happen. These spaces of geological relevance would not require us to build much. It would just be about how we curate the space. We recently got an invitation to curate in caves in the United Arab Emirates. This structure is already there. The hardware is there.

Nature has provided these galleries.
KK Absolutely. And we have been too lazy going a hundred miles an hour, creating these huge buildings with large carbon footprints. For too long we have ignored the original spaces that are there in abundance, tied into communities. That is for us the perfect balance. From our experience, the communities that surround the caves have the historical knowledge that would allow for a close engagement with relevant topics and curatorial exercises with them.

Given concerns about ecology, is there any justification for new buildings? There are so many existing sites and buildings available.
SM No, I don't think so.

That's a pretty big statement coming from an architect.
SM We have struggled with some students who don't understand that. One thing Kabage says all the time is, when a client brings a project, you should question whether it even needs to be a building. That is a realm architects need to start thinking about. Architecture is one of the biggest contributors to climate change. We have to start being a bit more responsible, and not just in regard to climate. This is a question I want to ask an architect who wants to create a masterpiece: Have you thought outside of your ego?

So with all this in mind, not just in the African context, how would you define a museum?
KK It is not what it used to be. Both its software and its hardware need to fundamentally change. The museum was an institution that embodied a lot of trauma. It was complicit in the colonial and imperial project. It needs to become extremely diverse, and I think that is happening. Fundamentally, the institution is going through a crisis. This is not a sharp and short exercise. Architecture is, in fact, at the root of questioning the museum. We need to develop the ability to embed the institution in society. In Kenya, we have dozens of tribes, each of whom have experienced colonization in multiple ways. How does the museum grapple with that? It's not a simple affair, but it is opening up an opportunity.

SM My definition of the museum is a place that is inclusive and not specific to a particular place. If I am somewhere in a village in Kenya, I can access the same information that someone deep in Argentina is accessing in terms of a curated museum. It is decentralized.

I would like to come back to this idea of a space where the community is actualized. Can today's museums do that?
KK With the community in mind. And it needs to be where the community is physically located. Museums are institutions of power and economy. As soon as they are centralized, they become about what you have extracted from the communities and brought back to the so-called museum, with its grand architecture. Once you dismantle that centralization, you open up the museum to all the nuanced context of where the museum resides. We are trying to do that at Suswa, in what you nicely referred to as actualized community space. We unashamedly introduce this new institution as the most critical evolutionary iteration of the museum of the future, in this, our putrid age of crisis, the so-called Anthropocene.

How should the process of designing museums be different?
SM We have thought about creating what we would call *BRIT*, for "Benevolent Reparations Institute." It would address all those complex issues around whom you are repatriating to, who gets the money, what it is used for. We envision going into the communities, presenting the problem, and letting the community come up with how they want the issues addressed. A panel of stakeholders, community leaders, museum curators, would discuss the proposals, and the best approach, if one could call it that, would be the one that gels with the majority. That one would be funded. We see this kind of institute operating everywhere, starting in Africa, to address not just what was looted, but how the communities involved could deal with the consequences of those actions today.

You have made your thoughts about deconstructing colonial models very clear. But for most of Africa the colonial era is now past. The future is about new challenges—technology, climate, pandemics. What comes after the decolonization project?

KK Unfortunately, it is a past and indeed present predisposition that continues to haunt us. With that said, one of our projects, the Maasai Cow Corridors, offers a hint at how we look to addressing this history and the present at the same time. We call it the reverse future. For thousands of years the Maasai lived with their cattle, before being displaced by the British colonial administration from their homelands. Today's neoliberalist pressures continue to sideline them. We began to think about an infrastructure that would allow them to come back to the city and maintain that connection, because it is their right as the original keepers of the land. We designed a rainwater-collection reservoir using cave geometry, an oasis where the Maasai could water their cattle and wild animals can find shade and refuge.

This thinking was informed by the urgency of human-induced climate change. At Suswa we are trying to do much the same, with proposals such as VHS, the Volcanic Steam Harvester, that allow people to not only elevate their status but also create a museum environment where people can feel at home. In a nutshell: Such projects are born through a thinking of reverse futurism, which intertwines the past into the present and projects into the future using a mix of the two.

SM Extraction is still going on. But now the climate crisis is putting everyone on a more level playing field. For too long, Africa had been playing at the bottom of the slope, so we could never get to the top of the hill. The future is about leaving that behind, so we are all at par and decisions are made collectively. At the core of our challenges is the realization that no one should come to the table with a higher authority or an "I know better than you" attitude. We need to be at the same level. We should discuss and agree, without any coercion.

1. Kabage Karanja and Stella Mutegi, "The Anthropocene Museum: Tracing our Decolonial Architectural Movements of Resistance in Africa," in *Slow Spatial Reader: Chronicles of Radical Affection*, ed. Carolyn F. Strauss (Amsterdam: Valiz, 2021).
2. Kabage Karanja and Stella Mutegi, "Profile: The Anthropocene Museum: A Troublesome Trail of Improvision Towards the Chthulucene" in *Design Studio Vol. 4: Working at the Intersection: Architecture After the Anthropocene*, eds. Harriet Harriss and Naomi House (London: Riba Publishing, 2022).

ROTH – EDUARDO NEIRA
Roth Architecture, Quintana Roo, Mexico

NATURE IS A PERFECT MUSEUM EVERY TIME

After driving two hours due east from the Mayan ruins of Chichén Itzá in the dense jungle of Mexico's Yucatán Peninsula, you may find yourself in a cultural space that challenges all the conventions of Western architecture. Visitors must remove their shoes to step inside. Built by hand with ancestral techniques and materials sourced from the surroundings, the undulating walls of SFER IK envelop a structure that relies on no plans other than spaces left open by the trees. Floors and surfaces are covered in harvested *bejuco,* a native plant. The works on view may be made by local artisans or celebrated artists. A love letter to the beauty and resourcefulness of nature, SFER IK is the vision of architectural autodidact Eduardo Neira, or Roth, as he is called. It is the fruit of playful, intuitive creativity unshackled from institutional constraint, and a reflection on the human condition at the edge of climate oblivion.

ANDRÁS SZÁNTÓ *Your AZULIK Tulum retreat on the Yucatán*
Peninsula inspired this conversation. Its exhibition space,
SFER IK, which you call a "museion," is unlike any I have seen.
Can you briefly describe it?

ROTH I started building my first cabin by the sea using rustic
nails. I was making my own nest, like a bird, using materials
from here and there. I had no money, and I learned how to live
in the jungle using only materials from it. The people who live
here don't use any materials made by machines. I made a home,
a hotel, and then our first museion, SFER IK, on the coast of
Tulum. Now we are making three of them around the world. Our
third one, a museion of contemporary art, will open in May 2023.

I didn't study architecture in a formal way. I tried to work by
following certain rituals, asking permission from nature. Where
there was water, we would leave the water. I never used precon-
ceived ideas. I just looked for spaces between the trees. I have
around two hundred trees living inside my home, and there
may be as many inside the museion. It is a process of incorporating ourselves into nature. When I started to make a
museion in the middle of the jungle with no money, some
thought it was a crazy idea.

I am curious, how did you develop your own style?
If you learn from nature, everything is easy. It is a natural and
intuitive path; here in the Yucután, many members of the construction team—locals from the Mayan communities—never
had the opportunity to attend school, and today they are on
their way to becoming architects. They are now working elbow-
to-elbow with people who worked with Norman Foster. These
guys have the wisdom of their hands. They have a relationship
with the elements. They are strong because they belong to
ancestral communities.

When people go outside their area of expertise, there will
be many surprises. We have twenty different initiatives now in
eleven industries, and people move from one area to another.
Our chef is working with the fashion department on edible
dresses. They are making dresses that grow as you use them.
These things only happen when you create a space of possibility
without concepts, and you play.

How would you describe the values that shape and guide all these activities?

We honor the obstacles we find. We think problems are masters that we can learn from. One day we were making, without plans, a concrete structure for a house. There was a hole in the wall, and one of the architects said that it was for an entrance. I told him that this was a problem we would leave for later. I think we need problems in order to grow, so the solutions will be unique. "How will you get in the house?" he asked. I said, "We don't know yet, and you don't need to worry."

We ended up with an entrance that is eight meters above the ground. You arrive via a bridge. Such ideas don't happen in a planned process. When you leave a problem for tomorrow and play in an irresponsible way, letting ideas go through you, then you can midwife miraculous things. But you have to trust your intuition and let the talent of your hands guide you through it.

That is more or less diametrically the opposite of most people's idea of architecture.

Not only of architecture—of life. The nonsacred way of thinking leads from concept to form. You end up optimizing everything into a square, and you live in a squared space, travel in squared cars, study in squared school, and end up with a square mind. However, if you do it the opposite way, and let form determine function—as it had been in the past, and as happens in nature—then you get the right result. This is why we never make a plan for our buildings.

Who are your influences or references for this uniquely organic, natural way of building?

We need to remember our position in nature. The only way I learn is through my experience with nature. I don't read or study architecture. I am interested in learning directly from the source—and the source is nature. If you put water at the center, a seed will grow, a community will grow, wonderful things will happen. But in our society we forget the community, we forget the elements, and we work only from our minds. We have to go down to the heart. And the heart only opens when it is in contact with the natural elements.

So you made a museum in the jungle. I'm curious why.
First, as you noted, I don't call it a museum; I call it a museion.
A museion is the place where the muses sit. The muse does not
necessarily sit in a church or a temple or even a museum—it
can sit in the middle of the jungle. We have here a project for
a community in the jungle. The actual form of the museum is
just an institutional idea. The concept of these institutions has
completely lost its power and is ultimately disappearing. People
are not interested in the form of the institution as we know it.
My idea was to create a space where an experience could take
place and where people could be inspired—a space that could
enhance people's ability to play. And naturally, people would
find their own creativity; that is a human necessity.

How do you choose artists to exhibit?
I never do that by myself. I have good curators helping me.
Things happen in a magical way with artists who get involved in
a deep way, like Tomás Saraceno and Ernesto Neto. We also have
artists in residence investigating Mexican rituals, and we will
soon have a show with bees. Our curator, Marcello Dantas, has a
distinguished creativity. At the moment, we are working on the
creation of five to six museions; one will be immersed in water,
another built with salt.

*How, then, do you define a museum? What does this term
mean to you?*
It must be the place where you connect with the source. This is
the meaning of art. The "ar-" in the word *art*, like in *architecture*,
means to unite what is separated, to bring together—and therefore to reconnect with the source. A museum, like a temple or a
church, should be a place where you can reconnect. But nowadays, they are places where a lot of art objects are stored. They
are not alive. They do not allow visitors to create and have a true
artistic experience.

*Often the future hides in the past. Clearly, the needs of people
tomorrow will be different from today. What does museum
architecture need to unlearn to create spaces that can be this
vital source of connection, creativity, and play?*

We need museions where people can reconnect to their core place in nature. Through the study of ancestral communities, we find an architecture with meaning. Thus, we can find a lot of museions everywhere—in the jungle, in the desert, in the mountains. Modern architecture with its squared forms makes our minds, our institutions, and our civilization painful. We keep recycling pain, because out of pain you can only create pain, and this goes on and on.

We have decided to focus our conversation around the themes of nature and play, which are both present in your structures. How does playfulness figure into your architecture?
It has to be part of the process of conceiving, creating, and living in the architecture. Because everything outside of play-fulness is ego, and nothing good comes from the ego. So playfulness is essential to the process of discovering. If you don't play, you don't take risks. It implies a constant innovation and renovation. All the animals and birds are happy in the morning; everything is new, the world is born again. And it is in that instant when you have an opportunity. You must sing a new song for the first time. Not the old song, the old concept. It has to be completely new.

Do you know of any museums that are playful? Or do any other institutions serve as references or inspirations for you?
All the ancestral buildings of old times for me are perfect. You see in Africa a lot of structures that could be a museum, a church, anything—they are absolutely perfect. Because they have been done with meaning and inspiration and for the pur-pose of reconnection. This is what I admire. I prefer to focus on the perfect example—which is, again, nature. Nature is a perfect museum every time. Because it is in a state of permanent trans-formation. It has the capacity to transform and grow and adapt and learn, allowing those who participate in it to transform it.

This is how a museum should evolve: incorporating more of the community and involving the participation of artists with it, to co-create something we call an alchemical process of learn-ing. Creation is when something that was not planned happens, spontaneously, out of playfulness and confidence. All the artists who come here now are looking for the same thing: something ancestral, connected with nature, with community. The new generation understands that.

Your buildings are made of plants, wood, mud, stone—organic materials. How can museum architecture be reconciled with nature to avoid the waste and pollution associated with most construction?
We are now developing a design team that will help us make a variety of organic forms. We are working on architectural prefabrication, so we can ship structures anywhere in the world, and our tech team is currently working in a lab with sophisticated 3D machinery. This is how we can design something organic, like a museion: mold each part and put it in containers to travel the world. When it arrives at its destination, it can be displayed in a simple and economical way.

We ask ourselves about the use of organic materials that do not destroy the environment and about houses that don't generate trash, like in nature, where everything is useful. There is no trash in nature. We can also train people to make houses for themselves and by themselves using what we call trash, so they break the chain of creating trash and everything can become circular. Ancestral architecture was always organic and circular. It did not leave any traces.

This way of thinking about building is clearly coming back. Can you tell me about what this will mean for museums?
Does anybody have a right to destroy anyone's habitat? When you destroy a jungle or any natural habitat to make a museum, then that institution is built on a cemetery. Then you have a museum built on destruction, like those cities built on the houses or temples of native communities.

Over the past several hundred years, we focused on the mind and lost our senses and got disconnected. Now the only solution for museums, for architecture, and for civilization is to reconnect with playfulness and joy, to all the beautiful things in nature. This is what I believe in, and I will try to share this message as much as possible through creations, structures, spaces, immersive atmospheres, and museions. This is how we echo the voice of nature and create a community with different, living foundations.

What are the unique challenges of working in this way? Maybe the parameters you have set for yourself are helpful, because they narrow down your range of options.
I discovered architecture only six years ago, and I explored materials along the way. We are developing a lot of new processes. An example: I wanted to make a concrete dome to play Tibetan bowls under. The authorities said, "No, the concrete won't look nice on the beach." "You can't make a *palapa*—it doesn't have good acoustics." And then I thought, "If we use the hexafoil form—a geometrical proportion: six around one, known worldwide as being sacred—then it will be possible to build a structure from top to bottom, with poles." The construction, therefore, would progress from the top to the bottom. The members of the construction team thought I was crazy. They said it was impossible, but I always see this word as a challenge. And that was the moment where I discovered my love for architecture. Changing all the concepts made me free.

My goal is to discover new technologies and new uses for materials every day. Now we are studying more than twenty materials, from the most technological ones used by NASA to the most basic ones. Our research-and-development team is working with different labs around the world to build a museum out of salt. We still haven't figured out yet how will it be shaped or structured; what we know is that in two years it will have been created.

At LUMA Arles, in the South of France—a former center of salt production, which is in decline—they are developing construction products using salt, including beautiful tiles covered in stable salt crystals and large bricks made of salt. Are there other methods or materials you are currently experimenting with?
Bejuco, a type of vine, represents one-third of the biomass of the jungle. We use it to create structures and design details. The vines are constantly spreading, and when they start to strangle the trees, cutting them helps the jungle. Nobody was using the vine in Mexico until we started to use it in the museion. If you

cut it correctly, you don't kill it; you can harvest it, like bamboo. There is more than enough in the jungle, and due to pollution, its proportion among the jungle vegetation is growing, so it is good to take some of it out. We discovered this when we had no money to buy other materials.

This kind of resilience happens in the jungle. People use the materials that are accessible to them. The Asháninka of the Peruvian Amazon find two or three hectares and live there for two years, after which they burn everything down—the houses, the boats, clothes—and move five kilometers away, and then they do the same all over again. In the places they cut, new species are born for the jungle. Over hundreds of years, this destruction of a small part of the jungle has allowed and helped the growth of new species.

At the moment, we are developing a floating hotel. Through this process we are thinking about how humans can live in different environments, respecting them and discovering new materials, new ways of living outside of the paradigm. To do so, we first have to get out of the hypnosis. We are a hypnotized society. We have to awaken and start seeing what surrounds us, because possibilities and materials for a new way of life are all around us.

You clearly have a different approach to building things, including museums, from what is taught in architecture school. What advice would you have for aspiring architects who wish to work in a truly ecological and community-driven way?
First, to learn from nature. Then, to play with their hands, trust in that intuition, and get involved with their surroundings. Coexist to co-create. With all beings, with all environments. Something special that we have in our team is the openness to learn, share, and discover one another. Different backgrounds and experiences merge. There are people who come from big architectural firms from all around the world, and local people who teach them their techniques and share their sensibility toward using the hands. Maybe the architect has an idea that hasn't explored the possibilities the hands can bring, and maybe the artist of *bejuco* has an idea that hasn't been sketched or modeled. Both have to ask themselves, "What can I learn from him? How can I develop that technique?"

We now have a team of topological architects who are working with local ceramists on ways to shape organic forms with computers. There is a lot of collaboration. This is a sign of our times: We can collaborate between ancestral and technological realms, young and old people together, to create a space of playfulness. That is the meaning of the museum for me—people across generations playing together to find new solutions.

This is all quite new, even for you. What in the end have you learned from your cultural projects and experiments? How are they pushing you in new directions?
I spend a lot of my day in a nest surrounded by trees, working on my computer. I try to learn how nature resolves situations. A hurricane not long ago broke the branches and the trunk of a tree. We were afraid we would have to remove the tree, but not even one leaf died. The tree just started sprouting new branches. Life is resolving the most complicated situations all the time. We just have to learn from it.

We can recover this ability to find solutions that are respectful of the environment, that are harmonic, that don't create trash—as long as we pay attention to nature. So what I try to share with young people is: Pay attention. Trust your own hands and your own power. Let the forms go through you. Forget the past. Forget what you have learned. Forget everything and start something new.

LIAM YOUNG
Southern California Institute of Architecture (SCI-Arc),
Los Angeles

WE ARE STILL STRUGGLING WITH DEFINITIONS

Where will museum architecture go next? Part of the answer lies in where we're all going—the still uncharted realm of digital experience. Making spaces out of pixels raises a host of questions for museum design: Should they follow the conventions of traditional museums? Must they have floors and walls, or pretend-gravity? Networked museums for digital artifacts may not need centralized locations at all. A whole new design language is waiting to be invented and implemented. It has few established practitioners, but if there is one, it is Liam Young. The Australia-born and Los Angeles–based artist, writer, documentary filmmaker, game designer, and architect teaches the ins and outs of worldmaking at SCI-Arc, the independent design school founded as an alternative to traditional architecture programs. Museum architecture has much to unlearn as it moves into this new era, Young contends. And it may invent some of the most exciting incarnations yet.

ANDRÁS SZÁNTÓ *You don't make physical buildings. You have done science fiction, game design, and documentaries. The BBC has described you as "the man who designs our futures." And you teach about digital space. How do you define your practice?*

LIAM YOUNG I describe myself as a speculative architect. I don't design buildings as physical objects, but rather I tell stories about how technology is changing our lives, spaces, and cities. These are no longer shaped only by the physical spectrum of architecture. The fixed, permanent infrastructure has been displaced by access to the network—software systems, algorithmic governance, and mobile technologies. To a large extent, networks now shape our spatial and urban experiences. So if architects want to remain relevant, then they need to start designing within these new contexts and systems. The traditional mediums with which architects work need to be reimagined.

Tell me about SCI-Arc and the course you coordinate there.
The things I'm describing used to be thought of as being on the margins of architecture. Now, architects who define themselves as shapers and makers of buildings are the ones on the margins. Today's architecture-school graduates don't necessarily become those kinds of architects. I created a program that embraces the idea that an architect may never work in an architecture office. They might become a game designer, a filmmaker, a storyteller, a consultant for a tech company. This necessitates a different education.

World-building is a vast field at the intersection of storytelling, design, and entertainment. Can you lay out the essentials?
You can't design for a single site anymore. You can't just think about the physical footprint of a building. You need to think of all the networks and entanglements, on a planetary scale, within which this building exists. We are part of a planetary-scaled city. A site that exists on a planetary scale has to deal with the flows and ecosystems we are caught up in.

World-building deals with all of that complexity. It imagines a building not just as a physical object, but as part of the entire world: the flows, the systems, the narratives, the cultures that exist through and around it and act upon it. But the building also shifts and changes. This is the kind of expansive practice we need to engage with the complexity of the world we are in.

Given that way of looking at architecture, tell me how you define the museum—the regular, physical museum.
For me, architecture is, at its core, the crafting of stories with and through space. Museum experiences are really the curation of those stories, organized through and around objects and collections of objects, as well as managing the visitor experience and visitors' understanding of those objects. Museums are the archives of the cultures that made them. They hold up mirrors to who we are and who we once were. Which means they also contain our past mistakes, biases, and triumphs. Those contradictions are crystallized in the containers those objects sit in.

The museums I connect with are not necessarily about the iconic envelope one travels through. They are more about the stories and narratives they contain. One of my profound museum experiences was in Daniel Libeskind's Jewish Museum Berlin, which I visited before it contained any objects. It was winter. There is a transition you make from the heated museum into the Holocaust void. You open a massive, weighted metal door; you need to use all your strength. You are hit by the cold air of Berlin as you walk into a massive chasm. The door slams behind you, echoing through this space. I had no idea of the envelope I was in. It was purely an architecture of sensation, all about the narrative of horror. That sticks in my mind.

Tell me what you think could be better about museums. How could or should they change to stay relevant?
My reservations are similar to those around traditional architecture. Museums struggle to reach broader audiences and become truly accessible. To a certain extent, the narratives of museum curators are screamed into an echo chamber. Museums are still relatively elitist, closed, and privileged institutions. They are good at talking to the sort of people who go to museums. That goes down to their curatorial missions and to their history, which has always been exclusionary and involved in supporting the privileged.

We're trying to get a grip on museums' digital future. The year is 2022. What about in 2052? What are your expectations of the future museum, which may be heavily digital and decentralized?
Museums will no longer just be fixed physical architectural experiences, curated by singular museum voices. They will also be remote. They will be digital. They will be dispersed and atomized across this planetary city. They will be more interactive. And they will be curated by visitors, audiences. What we are seeing as the beginnings of museums as backdrops to social-media experiences now, I hope will start to become more substantive, visitor-curated sets of experiences that will live both online and in an emerging set of fixed-reality experiences that exist outside the physical architectures of museums.

To fully grasp these possibilities, I would like you to take us inside the history of digital space. What are the precedents?
Think about what happened to public space. The market square in the village. The square in front of a church in a European city. The gathering around the campfire. These were forms through which cultures gathered to be together and share stories. They have all been physical, organized around the landscape and sources of warmth. And they have been defined and shaped by the architecture of either land, nature, or buildings. Until recently, that is how our culture has come together.

Now the dominant experience of being together happens online. The public spaces of cities have been supplanted by the public spaces of platform architecture. These are no longer managed by elected governments or tribal councils, but by a guy in a hoodie and sneakers, through rules defined by corporations. The public discourse of our world today exists in those online market squares, defined by the rules of commerce, shaped by algorithms that decide what voices get heard or suppressed. The nature of public space is now based on what we can describe as platform urbanism.

We can start to think about museums in a similar way. As they shift from being located around physical sites and architectures, they are evolving to become platforms.

As we shift to the virtual realm, what will be the enduring role of physical spaces?
Physical museums will become more like archives, tasked with the protection of objects. Visits to museums will be like pilgrimages to see the original. At the same time, physical museums will become layered with digital information. Digital doppelgängers of those same museums will exist on the network, as well as being dispersed within cities. Some digital objects will be geolocated. Museums will push out into the street as mixed-reality experiences. Architects will need to design not just the museum and its physical envelope, but also its digital doppelgängers and its digital shadows.

What are the muscles these architects will need to build, or the reflexes they have to resist to construct these experiences?
As a discipline, we are uniquely placed to engage with this layered, soupy mixed-reality world of the physical and digital. We just need a different material palette and a different set of rules.

We are currently trained to understand the structural system of concrete and steel and timber. We understand how light moves through a window. We understand scale and threshold and circulation. Now we will also need to understand the rules and metrics of the screen; we need to understand resolution, refresh rates, and what it means to design for machine-vision systems. We need to understand pixels as new mediums. We need to deal with the boundaries between the physical and the digital; what it means to put on a headset and turn on a screen and make that transition. We need to develop a new language of architecture that talks about those circulation experiences.

The people who make VR experiences are oftentimes film-makers. But VR, XR, MR, or whatever you call it has never really been a filmic medium. Film is about moving from frame to frame, twenty-four times a second. VR and mixed reality are not about frame-to-frame transitions. They are really about space-to-space transitions, from world to world. VR is therefore an inherently architectural medium. If we are willing to open up our practices to the digital, then much of our training will turn out to be already native to that virtual space.

So there is hope for architects. Is the metaverse the future of the museum? Or will it be more like gaming?

The metaverse is the future of everything, so it is also the future of the museum. And it includes the whole vocabulary of gaming. Gaming is the most complete example we have today of a hybrid digital reality. Phrases like *virtual reality*, *mixed reality*, *augmented reality* will disappear—it will just be reality. We are going to be able to dial up or dial down how much of our physical reality we choose to engage with at any moment. How much of the digital we choose to let in will be like channel surfing. Each of us will be able to tune the world to our own architectural and urban channels and curate the experience of that world.

When you look at early digital experiments for online galleries, so far they seem like a kind of fantasy Modernism, a simulacrum of the physical museum. Do you see this shifting?

We are still at the early stage. The first immersive digital experiences are mere decades old. They are still clunky. We are still attempting to replicate physical experience and traditional architecture. We need to develop a vocabulary for digital environments, a new way of conceiving these spaces. When we fully inhabit this mixed-reality world, the rules and the languages of the screen will become the rules and languages of architecture. The craft of design has to open itself up to the craft of code, game design, and platform infrastructure and engineering.

Interesting things happen in world-making and games. Players/participants can build, expand, and customize those worlds. They often have their own economies and currencies. Will some of this seep into the digital museum?

Totally. We see how communities are starting to form through and around blockchain technologies. A museum DAO (decentralized autonomous organization) will certainly emerge—and probably already has. These are the weak signals I would look for to understand how to think about communities that will be shaped and formed around museum experiences.

We already have the early DNA of what future museums will become. That DNA is not in the physical museum. It is to be found in these platform and blockchain communities. The rules

Liam Young

governing interactions there will become the rules that shape our interactions in the future museum.

A lot of effort is being put, in the real world, into creating a more social and flexible museum. In digital space these opportunities are wide open. Might we end up with a more fluid museum, something that is never pinned down? A natural-history museum in the morning, an art museum by day, an interactive digital gallery by night? A kind of shape-shifting museum?

We can imagine museums that do not need to have all their objects in one place anymore. Museums can focus less on the physicality of objects and more on experiences and relationships. Some of those will occur on site, in the traditional environment. But we can imagine objects being scanned and made digital in the most extraordinary resolution and detail. We can imagine digital editions that are as scarce and precious as the physical originals, where the aura of the physical can start to be attached to the digital objects at the same time. Then we can start to imagine museums moving out into the world. I can imagine guided tours in autonomous cars through streets with geolocated objects. I can imagine museums popping up in locations all over the world, made of digital editions.

But will they still be experienced as museums?
Those museums could become icons of digital space. Every generation has its own genre of architecture to which starchitects gravitate. Modernism had housing and the factory. The current generation, shaped in the 1990s, has the museum—that has been the pinnacle of the profession. But our generation's defining architecture is the data center.

The next generation's pinnacle of architecture may be defined by the sort of mixed-reality space we have been describing. In that world, museums may be digital spaces designed with the highest resolution and fidelity. When we go to the digital doppelgänger of the Guggenheim, it will be the most extraordinarily crafted, highest-bandwidth digital experience. But its collection might also exist as something that anyone can tune into and project in their own space. The Guggenheim could be in my bedroom.

Let's talk about gains and losses. What especially will digital spaces allow museums to do that they cannot today? And what will digital spaces lack that analog spaces do offer?
Technology is just a layer we drape across everything. It exaggerates our own contradictions and imperfections. The digital world is just as gate-kept and biased as the world that created it. I don't think that this move toward a more hybrid spatial experience is going to solve any of the problems we have now. So I don't know if we can think in terms of losses and gains. We need to look at what museums traditionally do well—which is to create a mirror that reflects who we are. And we need to understand what they do horribly—which is to observe cultures from narrow perspectives. We need to celebrate and mitigate those conditions in all the digital platforms and mediums through which the museum ultimately evolves.

Classical museums were machines to display classical mediums: painting, sculpture, drawings, and so on. New media fit uncomfortably in this envelope. So-called immersive experiences have emerged largely outside of museums. What is your view of them?
They are a continuation of the museum as spectacle, which has always been around, including in the form of the museum as a high point of architectural production. Immersive experiences are sitting on the same spectrum that museums have always occupied. But they are coming to a point where virtual-reality headsets are still clunky. The computational power to run real-time experiences, as opposed to the pre-rendered, fixed experiences like *Van Gogh: The Immersive Experience* is still not quite there. In the long run, the idea of going into a warehouse filled with eighty projectors and having digital experiences projected on the physical walls of that warehouse is something we will quickly move away from.

Where do you see hard constraints on the evolution of the hybrid institutions of tomorrow?
Our conversation about this ghostly digital museum doppelgänger has to acknowledge that it is powered by stacks of rare earth sitting in warehouses, connected to power stations. We need to think about how the software systems that will run

these museums are, at the moment, the intellectual property of five large, private companies that are not accountable to the public. We need to think about how that digital infrastructure could be imagined as a public utility, because that's exactly what it is. We need to think about code and algorithms as we think about access to fresh water and air. We saw in the pandemic that these systems are essential. These are just some of the shifts in thinking regarding the digital museum that have to happen.

I would like to end on a note of hope that the museum will remain an essential civic institution. You suggest it holds potential, as long as it is willing to adapt. Will digital architecture help maintain these institutions as essential places of gathering and storytelling, and as anchors of their communities?
Digital architecture will certainly help museums remain relevant as cultural archives. Because our culture is shifting. Artifacts no longer need to exist just in the physical world. And different types of cultural artifacts are being produced now. Digital architectures can help to value these new artifacts and preserve and maintain them. In the hypothetical Museum of the Internet, the first web page would be an important cultural artifact. At the moment we are just taking screenshots of these pages. But it is really the interactions, the connections, the networks, the entanglements, and the hyperlinks that are important. How do we collect all that in a way that is archival?

The technologies we're talking about are what I call before-culture technologies: They have evolved faster than our cultural capacity to understand them has. That is a difficult challenge for museums, which is why they have to a large extent dismissed or ignored these things until now. We are still struggling with definitions. Embracing digital architecture will help us catch up with how technology has already changed us.

The stuff we are doing now is still fragmentary, just the first infant steps. But you've got to start somewhere to explore.

The Dialogues
(all dates 2022)

Image Credits

Adjaye Associates
p. 128 Image © Adjaye Associates
p. 129 Top: Photo © Nic Lehoux;
Bottom: Photo © Alan Karchmer

Arquitetos Associados
p. 130 Rendering by Arquitetos
Associados
p. 131 Photos by Leonardo Finotti

BIG | Bjarke Ingels Group
p. 132 Photo by Iwan Baan
p. 133 Photos by Laurian Ghinitoiu &
BIG – Bjarke Ingels Group

Cave_bureau
p. 134 Photo © Francesco Galli,
courtesy La Biennale di Venezia
p. 135 Renderings by Cave_bureau

David Chipperfield Architects
p. 136 Photos © Simon Menges
p. 137 Top and middle: Photos
© SMB / Ute Zscharnt for
David Chipperfield Architects;
Bottom: Photo © SPK /
David Chipperfield Architects,
photo by Joerg von Bruchhausen

Diller Scofidio + Renfro
pp. 138–139 Photos © Iwan Baan

DnA_Design and Architecture
pp. 140–141 Photos by Wang Ziling,
© DnA_Design and Architecture

Frida Escobedo
pp. 142–143 Photos by Rafael Gamo

**gmp · von Gerkan, Marg und
Partners Architects**
p. 144 Photos © Christian Gahl
p. 145 Top: Photo © ATCHAIN;
middle and bottom: Photos
© CreatAR Images

Kerstin Thompson Architects
p. 146 Photos by Rory Gardiner
p. 147 Top: Photo by Derek Swalwell;
Bottom: Photo by Trevor Mein

Liam Young
p. 148 Photos by Liam Young
p. 149 © Liam Young

Lina Ghotmeh—Architecture
p. 150 Photo © Lina
Ghotmeh—Architecture
p. 151 Photos © Takuji Shimmura

MAD Architects
p. 152 Designed by Ma Yansong of
MAD Architects, image courtesy
of Lucas Museum of Narrative Art
p. 153 Photos © Iwan Baan

MASS Studies
p. 154 Photo © Kyungsub Shin
p. 155 Photo © Yousub Song

MVRDV
p. 156 Top: Photo © Ossip
van Duivenbode; Bottom:
Photo © Aad Hoogendoorn
p. 157 Renderings by MVRDV

NLÉ
pp. 158–159 Images by NLÉ

OPEN
p. 160 Top: Rendering © OPEN;
Bottom: Photo by INSAW Image

Roth Architecture
pp. 162–163 Roth Productions

SO – IL
p. 164 Photos © Naho Kubota
p. 165 Photos © Iwan Baan

Sou Fujimoto Architects
pp. 166–167 Photos by György Palkó,
© LIGET BUDAPEST

WHY Architecture
p. 168 Photo by Kevin Candland
p. 169 Photos by Steve Hall
© Hedrich Blessing Photographers

Acknowledgments

This is my second attempt to take stock of where the museum is going at a time of tumultuous change. As with the first, *The Future of the Museum: 28 Dialogues* (2020), its realization involved an extensive cast of characters.

First and foremost, I would like to thank the architects who sat through lengthy interviews, responded to multiple rounds of edits, and sketched original drawings to illustrate their dialogues. I am deeply honored and grateful for their ideas, time, and trust. I am also appreciative of the assistance that the colleagues of many of the architects provided. Architecture is always a collective effort, and so is a book.

This project would never have happened were it not for my Berlin friends Stephan Schütz and Doris Schäffler, who have been wonderful hosts and conversation partners about architecture ever since I first met Stephan while on assignment in Beijing to write about a building of his. Lena Kiessler's advocacy and optimism, now as ever, has been indispensable. I thank her colleagues at Hatje Cantz for supporting the enterprise of reflecting on the evolution of museums and the art world.

I owe a debt of gratitude to the members of the working team: Emily Markert for managing the process and carefully reviewing every word; Caroline Callender for her excellent transcriptions; Laura Noguera for her steadfast commitment to and joy in this book, as in all our projects; and Guadalupe Lobeto, for helping to keep everything on track. Myles McDonnell brought his sterling copyediting skills and his preternatural calm under pressure. And Neil Holt once again created an elegant book design.

While architecture has been a lifelong passion of mine, I am deeply grateful for the handholding provided by three friends and colleagues: Aric Chen, Beatrice Galilee, and Hans Ulrich Obrist. Each of them guided me in shaping the book and, when necessary, made introductions. Countless other friends and colleagues offered their help and feedback along the way. An inevitably incomplete list would include Laurie Beckelman, Katharine Beisiegel, Damian Chandler, Michael Conforti, Jo Craven, Marcello Dantas, Clementine Deliss, Chris Dercon, Rhana Devenport, Marina French, Brian Kennedy, Sonia Lawson, Adam Levine, Bertrand Mazeirat, Lars Nittve, Adriano Pedrosa, Abhishek Poddar, Suhanya Raffel, Brent Reidy, Elizabeth Roberts, Antonio Saborit, Katrina Sedgwick, Calum Sutton, Phil Tinari, Storm Janse van Rensburg, Jochen Voltz, Marc-Olivier Wahler, Christian Wasserman, and Debi Wisch.

As always, I thank my wife, Alanna Stang, who is no stranger to writing about architecture, and my children, Lex and Hugo. Some of our happiest times are spent in museums, and after this project, we have many more to explore.

Author
András Szántó

Series Editor
Lena Kiessler

Managing Editor
Emily Markert

Project Manager
Fabian Reichel

Project Advisor
Laura Noguera

Project Assistant
Caroline Callender

Copyeditor
Myles McDonnell

Graphic Design
Neil Holt

Typeface
Arnhem

Reproductions
DruckConcept, Berlin

Production
Vinzenz Geppert, Thomas Lemaître

Printing and binding
Livonia Print, Riga

Published by

Hatje Cantz Verlag GmbH
Mommsenstraße 27
10629 Berlin
www.hatjecantz.com
A Ganske Publishing Group Company

ISBN 978-3-7757-5276-3 (Print)

ISBN 978-3-7757-5277-0 (e-Book)

Printed Latvia

The design of this book's cover draws inspiration from Le Corbusier's seminal study of color, *Architectural Polychromy*.